BE IN ONE
Peace

DISCLAIMER

All information including techniques, exercises, therapies, medicines, nutrients, and herbs contained in this publication is general in nature and is intended for use as an educational aid. It does not cover all possible uses, actions, precautions, side effects, or interactions, nor is the information intended as medical advice for individual problems or for making an evaluation as to the risks and benefits of taking a particular substance or doing a particular exercise. The information contained herein has been devised without reference to cultural, dietary, societal, linguistic, prescriptive, or dispensing conditions which might affect the information provided.

Joanne's Websites: www.drjoannemessenger.com
www.beinonepeace.com

BE IN ONE
Peace

Essential Skills for Thriving in the New World

DR JOANNE MESSENGER

BALBOA.
PRESS

A DIVISION OF HAY HOUSE

Cover Logo: Margaret Lee

Balboa Press books may be ordered through booksellers or by contacting:

Balboa Press
A Division of Hay House
1663 Liberty Drive
Bloomington, IN 47403
www.balboapress.com.au
1-(877) 407-4847

Printed in the United States of America.

ISBN: 978-1-4525-0186-4 (sc)
ISBN: 978-1-4525-0187-1 (e)

Balboa Press rev. date: 05/16/2011

To all who wish to know more

"Use it wisely. Use it well." (Master Chiron)

TABLE OF CONTENTS

FOREWORD

I have known Joanne for over 20 years. She is one of the most exceptionally talented healers on the planet. She combines her highly refined intuition and perception with her vast array of skills and techniques. Her healings operate on all levels of your being—physical, mental, emotional and spiritual. It is wonderful that she has at last put pen to paper and shared her remarkable gifts and insights.

This book is beautifully written. Joanne conveys so many fantastic techniques, the majority only requiring the use of your mind and hands in a very simple way.

I highly commend this book to you.

Ian White
Founder of the Australian Bush Flower Essences

1. Why Do You Get Sick?

Health Is Your God-Given Birthright—or Is It?

Good health is a basic prerequisite for a comfortable life; yet it's elusive to many people. Whether it's the common cold that visits two or three times a year or the life-challenging diagnosis of cancer, health is a pervading issue in our world.

Clearly, however, disease isn't the problem. The problem is the lack of health. Cold bacteria and viruses cannot thrive in a healthy body. Cancer cells cannot thrive in a healthy body.

Darkness is an absence of light. Poverty is an absence of abundance. Cold is a lack of heat, and disease is a lack of health. Disease is a health deficiency, and it comes from dis-ease—which simply means "a lack of ease."

Ease means effortlessness and no resistance, and no resistance means going with the flow. When you resist and block the natural flow of your life, you create dis-ease.

Your Dis-ease Is Your Cure

If you have low self-esteem and feel life isn't sweet, it's a natural response of your body to seek out sweetness. You will crave sugar in order to put sweetness into your life. If you do nothing about raising your self-esteem and noticing how sweet life really, is you will continue to spiral into more and more sugar consumption and can even create rampant diabetes.

Likewise, if you have rigid thinking and lots of rules, your body will become rigid, too. If you do nothing about being more tolerant in your thinking, you will have no choice but to create arthritis in your body. If you want a flexible body, you need to have a flexible mind—and vice versa.

If you need to "put the brakes on" and take a break and you refuse to do so, you'll break a bone or blood vessel. If you don't consciously organize a break, you will create it unconsciously. It's as simple as that. One way or another, you will get your break. Broken bones and blood vessels will give you the break you want. They are the cure for not taking a break.

Disease is the cure for the life you are living.

Disease is the result of the way you live, think, and function. Use disease and illness as a clear guide as to what you need to change and where you need to change it. Look forward to where and how you choose your life to be.

Stop trying to restore your health back to where it was. *Where you were is where it all started!* As long as you focus on the past, you can't move ahead, and *if you don't change your direction, you'll end up where you're headed!*

Everyone is born with a purpose. Ultimately, we all have the same purpose of finding acceptance and living in love; however, many roads lead to Rome, and we all get to choose the route we travel to get there.

When you live in love, you live in peace. Inner peace and outer peace are then yours. Peace has always been your natural state; it just got buried under layers of life experiences. When you live in love, duality doesn't exist. Nor do separation, judgment of right and wrong, or resistance. If you fight against duality, however, it can certainly feel like you're separate from everyone and everything else. Within duality, there is always more duality, so the more you see yourself as separate, the more separateness you create. I'm sure you've noticed this with religions, governments, companies, and families. Where people disconnect and create separateness, they create factions within factions.

When you live in oneness, ease, and flow, there is no judgment of right or wrong. There is acceptance instead. When you live in oneness, you can see the gift in every experience:

- The broken leg that slows a person down so they don't have a heart attack.

- The cancer that tells the person where their bitterness or anger is stored and waves a flag so they can see where they need to heal.
- The flu that allows a person to rest and release the corresponding physical toxins from his or her toxic emotions, thoughts, and beliefs.

Do You Listen?

- *Do you listen?* Do you rest and release, or do you soldier on and cling to your old patterns?
- *Do you let the tail wag the dog?*
- Your body is a finely tuned, guided projectile designed to steer you through your life on a homeostatic mission. When you are on target, on purpose, and doing what is right for you, your body functions smoothly. When you wobble off course, get distracted, or do things that are damaging to your life mission, your body will let you know.
- The question is this: do you listen when your body is speaking to you?
- If you need a break, do you take one—or do you wait until you break something? Can you justify the rest then? Well, why couldn't you justify rest before, when you felt tired and your body was talking to you?
- If your shoulders are tense, do you stop and listen to what your should-ers are saying to you? *Your shoulders are your should-ers.* What is it you think you should have done or not done? Are there things you think you really should have done but haven't got around to yet? If you really ought to have done something, then get on and do it. If it's not something you ought to have done, then stop telling yourself you should and let the tension dissipate from your shoulders.
- If you have a pain in your neck, who or what do you think is a pain in the neck? Are you monitoring what you judge? The judgment causes you to wobble off your mission of acceptance and oneness. It creates pain, and your body tells you so you can resolve the issue, correct your programming, and get back on course.

If you break a bone and don't take a break, you're not listening. If your shoulders are tense and you're still telling yourself what you should or shouldn't have done instead of getting on with it, you're not listening. If you have a pain in the neck and you continue to judge, you're not listening. The break will take longer to heal than expected, or you'll break something else; your shoulders will get tighter and tighter; and your neck will become more painful until you listen and make the changes you need to make.

If you're driving along in your car and the oil light comes on, does it makes sense to simply cover the warning signal with tape? Of course not! It takes the red signal away, but it does nothing to solve the problem with the oil. If the problem isn't fixed at its source, the consequences can be dire—and probably very expensive!

If you take painkillers to take away the pain in your body, you are doing the equivalent of covering over the oil warning light. Pain is your body's signal to you that something is wrong. The problem needs to be corrected at its source—or else the consequences can be dire. Your body has the wonderful ability to heal itself within certain parameters, so more often than not, you don't realize the importance of correcting the real problem. If your engine seized within twenty minutes of getting the pain, you would surely get the message—but your body has the amazing ability to adapt. So rather than you breaking down there and then, your muscles tighten a little more to try and keep things stable, and your nerve system dulls down the pain signal after a time so you don't hurt. But what if those same nerves control your heart, gall bladder, or bowel? Your body is an excellent guidance system, and it can be very expensive if you continuously ignore what it tells you.

Every time your body sends you a pain signal—whether it's from a nerve, muscle, bone, or organ—it is signaling you to adjust your course and get back on track. The sooner you correct and put systems in place to not keep repeating what caused the concern, the smoother the ride—and the better your health. The longer you take and the more resistant you are to doing what is innately right for you, the bumpier it will get.

If you leave it past the point of difficult return, your engine will seize!

Exercise

When you notice a symptom:

1. Stop
2. Take inventory
3. Take a different action or behavior

As you re-train yourself to start listening to your body again instead of overriding its signals, you will realize that pain and discomfort are your best friends. They are direct communications from your body, telling you that something is not right.

Every time you receive a message from your body that says *stop*, take inventory, and change your behavior or the direction you are going. Get closer to living your life from your own centre. The dog will start to wag the tail again.

Steer your course in accordance with the guidance from your soul rather than submitting to the whims of your ego or personality that says, *take a painkiller, have a cigarette, eat a cookie, have a drink,* or whatever other means it uses to dowse your internal guidance system.

2. What Put You Back on Course?

You're sauntering down your road of choice in your finely tuned, guided mission vehicle on your journey called life, and you have a malfunction. Being the self-responsible, self-correcting, self-healing model you are, you assess your situation and consider what has happened and what needs to be done to rectify the situation as best you can before you continue on your journey.

You realize the malfunction is a gift. It's a self-monitoring device that is on all the current models of humans. It lets you know immediately that maintenance is required.

You know already that painkillers are only going to mask the real problem. You set about discovering what is required for true healing rather than symptom management.

You find the cause of the concern, follow through with what is required, and thank the issue that alerted you to the need for maintenance and self-correction. You understand that you may have gone way off course without this monitor in place and extend your gratitude to it.

You continue to saunter down your road of choice ...

Isn't this an easier road than allowing yourself to be in pain or get a disease and then try and find a cure? Your body will give you warning signals long before any major symptoms or challenging diagnosis. It will give you the opportunity to adjust and maintain as you go.

Have your illnesses and injuries interfered with your work schedule or social pleasure? Have you recognized your unconscious (or rather, higher conscious) way of getting you back on course?

"Oh my gosh, he's ignoring himself—a gentle bump on the right shin should do the trick."

"Oh dear, he's ignoring himself again—a harder bump on the right shin should do the trick."

"Okay, he's still ignoring himself—a right shin break should get him to take the break he needs."

Rather than injuries taking you off course, they are actually trying to keep you *on* course.

When you have injuries on the right side of your body, your body is telling you that something you are *doing* needs adjusting. You either need to change what you are doing or the way you are doing it.

Conversely, when you have injuries on the left side of your body, your body is telling you that something you are *thinking* needs adjusting. You either need to change what you are thinking or your perspective on it.

Your ego wants to run the show and thinks it's been hard done by and delayed if you have an injury or an illness, when really, injuries and illnesses are blessings you would do well to be grateful for. Without the constant reminders to maintain your balance and get back to the middle of your path, you might waste your time and energy on ego-driven tangents.

The trick is to stop, take inventory, and make the corresponding adjustments to your thoughts, beliefs, and behaviors as soon as you notice!

Are They Challenges or Gifts?

What are the events in your life that have endeavored to get you back on course? Often these gifts may have been cleverly disguised as major challenges:

- Did you have an illness?
- Have you had many bouts of the same illness?
- Have you had multiple illnesses?
- Were you injured?
- Have you had any surgery?
- Have you required medication for any reason?
- Did your parents divorce?
- Did you move house a lot as a child?
- Did you change schools frequently?

- Was something or someone taken away from you?
- Did you feel you were the odd person out in any situations?
- Were you discriminated against for any reason—perhaps race, sex, or gender?
- Did you suffer abuse in any way?
- Did you have any physical characteristics or afflictions that set you apart from others and made you stand out in a way that you'd rather they hadn't?
- What else?

Exercise

Many memories and insights will come to you, so jot them down as they bubble up.

1. Take a wide page and divide it into two columns.
2. List all the events you can remember down the left column. Don't write a huge essay about them—just a couple of keywords. Don't judge how many there are—just keep listing! Don't waste any time or energy feeling angry or hurt about anything—just keep listing!
3. Who are the people you would prefer to not share company with for any reason? Add them to your list, too. Keep listing down the left column. Get a bigger notebook, if you need, or use a computer—whatever your preference.

I'm guessing that most (if not all) the situations you have on your list have a serious tone to them. Chances are, you have mastered seriousness! You can decide to step into fun and enjoy the fulfilling changes that are available to you.

Rather than being so serious, you can lighten up your life by considering it to be something wonderful. For example, you could consider your life as "Mastering My Marvelous Mission," "The Taking Back My Power Project," "My Freedom from Foolery Venture," or "Embracing My Excellence Extravaganza." I know you can do better than this! Just make it fun.

4. Now it is time for the right side of your page. *What did you need from the situation you have listed on the left that you didn't get?* Write down a need for each situation. If you just write a generic answer like

"love," you're not going to get the full benefit that's available to you. Be more specific. For example, if you were five years old, hurt your foot, and cried all by yourself for an extended period, if what you needed was a hug, then write "a hug" down. If you were at a party and everyone got a balloon except you and what you needed was a balloon, write this down.

5. Complete your list and notice the common themes. Are there repetitive things you felt you didn't get? It's interesting, isn't it? Pay attention to what you are learning about yourself. This is truly a gift.

Now it's time for the fun part. Healing can not only be fun, it probably needs to be. *As long as you stay seriously attached to a person, situation, thing, time, place, or event, you're probably going to have a hard time letting it go. Allow yourself to have light hearted fun.*

Lighten up so you can brighten up.

6. Cut off the left column. This list has been very useful to you, has it not? Fold it in four and thank it—the situations and people involved. Burn the list and say that you release it and everyone involved with it. Just let it go. It's you who has been feeling hurt here, so put an end to it!

7. Keep your right list, which is the right list!

8. Start at the top of your right list, and *for the next thirty consecutive days, give yourself what you needed—and make it ridiculously fun.* For example, if you needed a hug, hug yourself in front of the mirror and pull ridiculous faces. If you needed a balloon, then go and get yourself one (or ten!) and have fun with them—regardless of what other people are doing around you.

9. Have as much fun with this list as you can. Notice how much better you feel and how much more energy you have.

10. Be discerning about the recurring things you need. Make certain you give these to yourself in the future. Don't wait until you feel they are missing. Create your life so that what you need is in place for you ahead of time.

3. Why Do You Like the People You Do and Not the People You Don't?

You just click with some people right away—and others you just want to keep right away from. Why is that? You've only just met someone, and within the first three seconds, you have made all sorts of decisions about him or her and how much you want him or her in your life—or not.

Broadly speaking, *we like the people who are like us and dislike the people who are different from us to the degree of sameness or difference.*

The things we have in common bring us together. For example, at a tennis club or meditation group, it's the thing that everyone has in common that brings them together—tennis or meditation.

The things that are different about us are the things that tear us apart (e.g., religion, skin color, or political alliance). What you see as the same or different simply depends on your values and what you see as important. Many of these values you embrace because of the geography of your birth, the religion of your parents, and even your parents' political persuasions. One of the blessings of maturity is the ability to re-choose from a conscious level what you place more value on. The great thing about childhood is that it's over. You can choose for yourself now.

If you notice the things you have in common with people, your rapport will grow. Likewise, if you notice and focus upon the things you don't have in common, you will lose rapport.

Practice with a loved one or friend. Whenever you're with them, notice the things you like about them, and put your attention on these things. What happens? How fast does it happen?

Notice what happens if you put your attention on the things you don't like so much.

Experiment gently. You don't want to lose a good relationship or friend over something you already know on some level.

Spread your wings and put your attention on the things you like about your acquaintances. Prepare to be amazed by how much and how fast your level of trust and bonding goes up. Can you see that when you do this with everyone, everywhere, every time, your affinity with people will grow and continue growing? This builds your feeling of connectedness.

If everyone across the planet noticed the things they had in common with everyone else and allowed this to blossom, there would be no wars. There'd be no need.

Start with your immediate circles of influence. Start putting your jigsaw pieces in place so you match the picture on the box—so you create the life you came here to live.

Notice what you like about your loved ones, family, friends, work mates, and neighbors. Then spread your circle wider to include people in shops, people in traffic, and the people in other areas of your life. Most importantly, include yourself. Notice the things you like about yourself, and focus on them.

Mirror

There are some tribes in the world in which people have never seen themselves in a mirror. The closest they have been to seeing their physical image is their reflection in water. They deduce with reasonable accuracy what they look like because of similarities with other tribe members—especially their family members.

When you want to see what you physically look like, you simply look at your reflection in a mirror. You can even stay there and fiddle with how you look until you are pleased with the results. If you plan to gain or lose weight, clear up your skin, or wear a smile, you simply look in the mirror and see how you're going. It's an instant and accurate monitor. This is easy.

What about your emotional reflection and your beliefs reflection? Where do you see these?

The people around you are your reflections. You will see in them what you have in yourself. The qualities you really admire in others are the same qualities you have in yourself. You could not see these qualities in the other person if you did not have the same quality in you. It cannot be reflected if you don't have it.

For example, if you notice and admire people who are generous and caring, then generosity and care are qualities that you yourself have. You could not notice these qualities in others if you did not have them yourself. You would notice other things instead—things that you did have; things that you are tuned in to. Other people are mirroring your own qualities to you. If your friends are inspiring, competitive, well-groomed, or patient, somewhere in the circumstances of your life, you too will display these qualities. You cannot recognize attributes in others if you don't have them yourself.

Have you ever had the experience of admiring someone for something, and someone else can only criticize them? The critic can't see the good qualities in someone if he or she doesn't have those particular qualities. The very characteristics the person is criticizing are ones he or she has and unconsciously sees reflected back.

Exercise

You'll need your notebook or computer again.

Make a list of all the qualities you admire about your:
* partner
* family members
* friends
* work colleagues
* neighbors
* acquaintances
* favorite actors
* favorite singers
* favorite writers
* leaders
* anyone who has attributes you like—whether fictional characters or real

Keep listing! Use as many pages as you can possibly fill. Include everything. Keep your lists handy so you can add to them regularly.

Every day for thirty consecutive days, choose an attribute from your list and embody it. Have fun with it.

For example, if you chose "generous" from your list, then have the most fun you can possibly have being consciously generous all day. Make a hot drink for someone with all the flair of a world-class barista; open doors for others while you wear your dental poster smile.

If you chose well-groomed, have fun being well-groomed all day. Iron your clothes with panache; enjoy sliding your tongue over your freshly brushed teeth; arrange your clothing as particularly as a catwalk model. Have fun with it *all* day!

If you chose fitness, have fun developing your fitness all day. Put music on and dance as you vacuum; do leg exercises under your desk; wriggle your earlobes while you wait for the train.

Consciously embody the attributes you admire. You actually have them already, so simply bring them to the surface in a fun and pleasurable way. You'll be amazed at how much more energy you have and how good-natured people become around you.

You'll love it so much you'll keep going past thirty days.

~~~

Mirrors are mirrors. *They simply reflect what is there,* and they aren't selective about it. A physical mirror will show you any extra padding around your middle just as accurately as it shows your gorgeous smile. It's simply up to you which bits you notice—or not.

Similarly, with your emotional mirrors, people around you reflect aspects you judge harshly just as dependably as the ones you respect. It's up to you whether you notice or. If you notice it, you can change it.

If you criticize yourself for something, you will criticize others for that very same thing. They reflect it back to you. They show you what you hide from yourself.

Every time you judge someone for anything at all, your mirrors show you what you have in yourself and may not see.

Naturally, it works both ways. You reflect to others what they have in themselves.

Exercise

1. Set up your page in three columns. If you orient your page landscape instead of portrait, you will have more space.
2. In the *left* column, make a list of all the qualities you dislike about your:

- partner
- family members
- friends
- work colleagues
- neighbors
- acquaintances
- favorite actors
- favorite singers
- favorite writers
- leaders
- anyone who has attributes you like—whether fictional characters or real

All the traits you have listed that you don't like in other people are actually your own traits. They are either traits you deny or traits feel you could not love yourself for if you had them. For example, if you judge someone to be arrogant, and you don't like arrogance, then that person is showing you that somewhere—whether you are conscious of it or not—you behave arrogantly.

The other person is showing you a part of yourself that you don't love—something you consider to be unlovable; therefore, you deny it in yourself.

If you listed impatience, somewhere in your life, you are impatient. You might be incredibly patient in many areas, but there will be an area in which you are impatient—perhaps repeating to an elderly person the same thing for the umpteenth time, children having tantrums in the supermarket, traffic jams, or bosses who are slow to give you a raise.

3.   In the *middle* column, answer the question, *Where do I do that?* for each of the irritating behaviors and traits you listed in the left column. For each characteristic you see in someone else that you don't like, ask yourself, *Where is this in me?*

If you don't see where you behave like this or hold that belief, then simply keep looking. It will be there somewhere, because if you can see it in others, you have it in yourself. Naturally, you hide it from yourself. The more you don't like the trait, the more you hide it; hence, the more you will see it in others to show it to yourself.

The higher part of you is working with you constantly to get you to see what you need to heal or change. You are being shown every single day. What's more, your loved ones can see where you need to heal and change as clearly as a neon sign—just as you can see where they can grow. We only hide it from ourselves. Everyone else can see it, because we reflect it to the world.

Allow yourself to know yourself better—without judgment. Be gentle with yourself. Everyone on the planet has an assortment of qualities. It's actually a little deluded to think that everyone has faults except you. Everyone is on a path of growth and acceptance, and at this time in our history, more and more are choosing to awaken and grow consciously.

If you think a trait is totally unlovable, you may totally bury it from yourself and absolutely refuse to see it. However, just because you don't see microwaves and electricity doesn't mean they're not there!

"Can't" usually means "won't." Rather than not being able to see something, you won't allow yourself to see. After all, you're judging the characteristic as not good, so why would you volunteer to admit this in yourself—unless, of course, you want to heal, grow, become more whole, and fulfill your life purpose on earth.

4.   Breathe into your heart, and be honest with yourself. Honor yourself in your process. This is not an opportunity to whip yourself further or to blame others. It's a chance to acknowledge what you hide from yourself and to recognize the gift of mirroring. When you

understand that what you project onto others is what they mirror back to you, you can clearly see which thoughts and behaviors to change.

If you have hidden the truth from yourself so deeply you truly cannot see where you display a particular emotion, behavior, or belief, ask someone else on the proviso you:

- Don't shoot the messenger
- Don't use the information to shoot the messenger at a later time
- Don't shoot the messenger

If you remain s-i-l-e-n-t, you may find it easier to l-i-s-t-e-n. Take note of the reflection of those words. If you argue or resist the message, you will miss the generous gift you are being shown and likely deter the person from giving you further gifts in the future.

If you are fortunate enough to have a loved one who is brave and secure enough in his or her own being to tell you what you won't even tell yourself, then consider yourself eternally fortunate to have this person in your life. Be very grateful!

Be mindful, though. If you ask others to show you what you can't or won't see yourself, there is a risk of giving your power away. Maintain your energy within yourself, and answer your own questions where you possibly can. Be responsible and accountable to yourself.

Notice the truth of your behaviors and beliefs, and don't judge yourself for them. Enlightenment means gaining light—not harshness.

5. Expand your awareness to encompass what you see in others; this is what you have in yourself. Fully comprehend the mirror philosophy and understand that *everyone in your life* is a gift, because they show you things about yourself that you may not have been aware of previously.

Allow yourself to have the behaviors or qualities you dislike—even if you would prefer not to have them. You don't have to change everything overnight. Remember the hare and the tortoise? It's the tortoise who keeps plugging away that wins.

Judging yourself as bad for having so-called negative qualities is the very reason you're hiding them from yourself in the first place.

This is just as harsh and equally as detrimental as judging someone else. There is always balance in the universe. There is day and night, summer and winter, happiness and sadness, and silence and noise. Allow yourself to be you—warts and all. Love yourself exactly as you are, and then see what more resourceful qualities you can replace these qualities with. Be the tortoise.

If someone mirrors something which you blatantly don't have, they are showing you that you wouldn't love yourself if you had that trait. For example, if you are slender and always have been, and you see someone who is obese and this appalls you, they are showing you that you couldn't love yourself if you were obese.

They are showing you the conditions you put on love—and in this case, the conditions you put on loving yourself. For example, *I can only love myself if I am slender* compared to *I love myself no matter what I look like.*

Unconditional love means no conditions—and this includes thin and fat. Ghandi was slender; Buddha was ample—yet both were remarkable and highly influential beings in our history. If you're not loving yourself because of your physical appearance, you're being shown an aspect which you judge. Once you are aware of this, you can let it go.

6. In your *right column*, list the positive polarity, or the antonym, of what you listed in your left column. For example, if you listed impatience in the left column, list whatever means the polar opposite of this to you, such as patience, in the right column.

The positive polarity of *stingy* might be *generous.* The positive polarity of *arrogant* might be *humble. Lazy/energetic. Rude/polite.* Use a thesaurus if you need help.

The right list is the right list. These are the qualities to enhance and grow within yourself. Make certain they are qualities you respect and desire. If you had something like *superior* in your left list and the antonym is *inferior,* make certain you have a preferable quality in your right list, such as *egalitarian, impartial,* or *fair.*

7. Cut off the left and middle columns (if you have done this on your computer, print it off), thank them, and bless them for what they have shown you. Burn them and let them go.

8. Keep your right list.

9. *For the next thirty consecutive days, choose a quality from your right list, embody it, and enhance it in your life.* Remember to have fun with it. Grow these qualities into massive oaks so there is no space for weeds to grow.

4. You Get More of What You Think About

You get more of what you think about. Your central nervous system is set up to support this. The reticular activation formation (some people call this the reticular activation system) in your brain helps you notice more of what you put your attention on. If you recently purchased a green car, all of a sudden, you'll notice green cars everywhere. If you or someone close to you is pregnant, you start to notice pregnant women everywhere. If you have a new tattoo, a diamond watch, a Chihuahua, or hay fever, you'll notice it everywhere until your focus fades. When you don't put your attention on it anymore, you will begin to notice more of what you have moved your attention to instead.

Use this to your advantage. *Think about all the things you like, and you'll see more of these things in your life.*

Where your life is today is determined by the choices you made in the past that brought you to this point. Similarly, the choices you make now will determine where your life goes in the future. The choices you make are a result of your beliefs.

To be precise, you create your life according to your *beliefs*. Your beliefs determine your *thoughts*, your thoughts determine your *words*, and your words determine your *actions*. In other words, *you create your life by what you think, say, and do.*

Have you ever engaged yourself in a self-improvement campaign by changing your actions, only to revert to your old ways when you got tired or distracted? Maybe you successfully gave up smoking or lost weight only to relapse at a later time. Often the setback happens when you're under stress and the subconscious patterns that you truly believe about yourself get airplay again.

When you make changes at an action or behavior level, the changes will only be successful as long as you keep up your new behaviors.

To have longer-lasting change, you can change your words—not only the words you speak out loud, but also the words you speak in your head. You can do this simply by monitoring your language and making sure it takes you in the direction you want to go. For example, say "I am smoke free" or "I am shedding excess fat" instead of "I am giving up smoking" or "I want to lose weight."

The words you use are a direct command to all the cells of your body to give you what you asked for—to specifically give you what you asked for, not what you thought you asked for.

If you want something, you get to want something. Rather than actually getting it, you get to keep wanting it. If you want to lose weight, you get to want to lose weight. Wanting something projects it into the future. Be selective about where you use the word *want*.

Also be discerning with how you use the words *I am*. Remember that the words you use are direct commands to all the cells in your body. They have no choice but to obey. If you declare *I am gorgeous*, then you are. If you say *I am smart*, then you are. *Whatever you state after* I am *is a self-fulfilling prophecy. It's a direct command. You have no choice but to create it in your life.*

If you say *I am stupid*, you have no option but to create it in your life. If you think *I'm too fat*, you have no choice but to create it.

Words out your mouth and words in your head determine your actions. If you think you're stupid, your actions will follow, and you cannot help but make mistakes. If you think you're too fat, you have no choice but to put food in your mouth—even when you've had plenty to eat.

Words and thoughts are affirmations. Choose them wisely!

Your beliefs and values set the template for how you think.

When you believe *I am smoke-free, I am gorgeous, I am successful,* or whatever else with as much conviction as you believe *I am male* or *I am female,* you will have it simply and easily. *Doubt is the saboteur;* it undermines you and prevents you from having what you desire.

If you doubt you can have it for any reason, you interfere with your manifestation.

I AM was the Hebrews' name for God and is even on the walls of Egyptian temples (Catherine Ponder, *The Dynamic Laws of Healing*. DeVorss Publications: 1966).

If you habitually state, "I am too young," "I am too old," "I am skinny," "I am fat," or whatever else, you will create it. It is a direct order to the god within you to create this for you. Your words are constantly building you up or breaking you down, healing you or harming you.

Ensure your language is filled with positive *I am* statements such as:

- I am healthy
- I am beautiful/handsome
- I am prosperous
- I am abundant
- I am peaceful
- I am loving
- I am lovable
- I am strong
- I am worthy
- I am fertile
- I am happy
- I am successful
- I am grateful

Until you train your mind to be peaceful and still, it will chatter away for a large part of your waking hours. If it's going to chatter, then give it something positive to chatter about. Instruct it to say affirmations of your choosing. Make absolutely certain your beliefs, thoughts, and actions are working for you and not against you. Consciously choose what you think, say, and do.

Your Brain Doesn't Recognize "Don't"

Your brain doesn't recognize *don't*. No matter what I say, don't think of an orange basketball with black stripes on it. No matter what

I say, don't think of a clear glass vase with fresh red roses in it. What happens? It's automatic, isn't it? Your brain goes ahead and creates the picture all by itself. Your words—whether you think, say, read, or hear them—are a direct command to create. The more direct the order, the more diligent the response.

Trickily, if you say you don't want to get fat, your brain doesn't recognize *don't* and sees it as a royal command to get you fat.

If say you don't want to spill your cup, it's as good as an instruction to tip the contents.

Change your words to support you. Think and say precisely what you desire rather than what you don't want.

For example:

- Instead of "Don't pig out on chocolate," tell yourself something like "I eat nutritious snacks."
- Instead of "Don't forget to buy the fruit," find a thought that can be more positively expressed as "Remember to buy the fruit."

Change the wording to suit yourself, such as:

- I eat carrots for snacks.
- I eat apples in between meals.
- I only eat at meal times.
- I drink plenty of fresh water daily.
- I have fun exercising every day.

Instead of "Don't lose your temper," try something like:

- I am calm and serene.
- I am relaxed and at ease.
- My life is peaceful, and my relationships reflect this.

Create affirmations that suit you. Make them your own. Take your power back, and be your own authority. You're the adult now. If you don't like your thoughts, change them to what you wish.

You are in charge of creating your life, so make it according to your ideal self and the life you choose rather than settling for crumbs.

Consciously Create Your Own Reality

The circumstances of your life are no accident. The choices you made and the actions you took in the past determine your current state of affairs. This is commonly referred to as the Law of Attraction or "creating your own reality."

You have created the situations you're in and the experiences you have by the decisions you made. The choices you made and the thoughts you had last year and last week determine where your life is today. Hence, the thoughts you have today and the choices you make now determine how your life will be in the future. If you don't like where your life is heading, then you need to think different thoughts and make appropriate choices to get you where you really want to go.

If you don't like where you're headed, change your direction.

Naturally, it helps immensely if you are clear about what that direction is.

Many influential people have reminded us of the universal Law of Attraction. They have brought into conscious awareness that you can attract whatever you choose by visualizing and focusing upon it. Napoleon Hill's book *Think and Grow Rich* has been repeatedly reprinted since 1937; Esther and Jerry Hicks' book *The Law of Attraction* is likely to go the same way. Most westerners are familiar with the quote from the Bible, "As a man thinketh, so is he." These (and many others) are purporting the significance of what we think, say, and do and how we can consciously use our thoughts, words, and actions to attract our desires into our lives and create the lives we want.

With all this knowledge, why are there still so many unhappy, sick, and impoverished people? Why hasn't everyone been able to manifest all of life's comforts and pleasures?

The Law of Attraction is also known as the Universal Law of Sacred Resonance. It is the universal law that magnetizes and draws all back on their path to Source. It allows all aspects of your soul to be drawn back into the heart of your soul. As you attune to the Law of Attraction or Law of Sacred Resonance, your heart will open and allow the opening of your energetic pathways that connect you to the multi-dimensions of Source. This, in turn, allows you to reclaim your soul fragments back into oneness.

Perhaps there is a higher purpose to this knowledge. When you are attached to outcomes, you are not open to receiving all the universe can bring to you. Allowing all the universe can bring you rather than attracting what you can think of from your limitations of thought is equivalent to *being* instead of *doing*. We aren't human doings; we are human beings.

One of our missions while we're here on earth is to remember who we are—to remember to *be*. When we continuously *do* and fill our lives up with more distractions, it is easy to end up doing even more and neglect our natural state of being.

To manifest your goals, visualize them as clearly as you can, and *feel the feeling as if you've already achieved the goal*. You'll be in the driver's seat. This works. However, it locks in the parameters of your choices rather than allowing the whole truth of who you are to express itself according to *what you came into this life to be*. It limits you to what you are visualizing. The higher plan of what we're here to achieve is often far more glorious than what our limited thinking considers we're worthy of.

When you align with your soul's purpose for being on the planet, manifestation comes from looking deep within yourself. *Go in, not out*.

When you are still in your heart and open up to the hearts of every man and woman, you will feel yourself as the divine. This doesn't mean you're claiming to be God. Divine means *de-vine*—no vines of attachment, no cords to your ego or fear, no strings attached—just the pure you.

When you allow yourself to go within the stillness of your heart, you open up to the higher or bigger plan for your life and role on earth. Rather than merely attracting a bigger TV screen or a longer limousine, consider aligning with your essence on your path of purpose. When you know you're within the being space of your heart, ask to bring through everything that is for your highest good. Ask for your spiritual path and the work you came here to do to come to you. *Use the Law of Attraction for your spiritual purpose rather than only the ego-driven needs or physical comforts.*

When you're within the quiet space of your heart, surrender to higher guidance. Allow yourself to receive and understand the gifts you are given.

Surrender to all that is truly your path. Let go of your attachment to outcomes and be free to receive.

If you feel disillusioned, you're in the way of your higher truth. Your mind is in the way. Go deeper within and ask where you're meant to be.

Consciousness is evolving. It no longer works the way it did previously. You used to be able to set a goal, achieve it, and move on to the next goal. You are now in a time of awakening to higher truths. You'll find these truths in your heart space—where you need to surrender in order to access them. You won't necessarily hear the guidance while in your heart. This is part of the letting go of control and surrendering. You may well hear the guidance when you're doing something else, like doing dishes or listening to music.

If you're not clear on whether an idea is from higher guidance or from your head because it's something you want to hear, then thank the universe and re-surrender. Let go the need to have whatever it is.

When you let go of attachment to the outcome, there is no need to make decisions, because what is truly right for you will stay, and what is not aligned with your highest good will drop away. You do, however, need to open the doors that are offered to you and step through with faith and confidence.

It's a bit like constipation. If your bowel tells you to go to the toilet and you put it off for whatever reason (inconvenient timing, not being at home and disliking public toilets, etc.), if you keep ignoring the messages, then pretty soon your bowel won't send you the message any more.

You now have the opportunity to live your life in accordance with the higher aspect of yourself.

When you eat, it doesn't work efficiently to eat a huge amount and then not at all for a month. Regular installments of good food will give you the best results. It's the same with surrendering. It's not like you surrender once, and that's it. You get to keep on surrendering. Allow yourself to go into the stillness every chance you get.

Solar Panels

Let's delve deeper into the law that what you think, say, and do determines what you manifest.

If you know you're a good singer, you will habitually think thoughts that support this. You will habitually support your belief, and it will be evident in your communication with others. You will habitually take steps that support your belief, such as practicing, taking lessons to fine-tune your talent, singing in the shower, singing in the car, performing in musicals, or even making recordings.

On the contrary, if a person believes they are a poor singer, they will think thoughts that support this. They will say unsupportive things about their singing ability in their head (and possibly out loud) when communicating to others—especially if asked to sing publicly. Rather than seeking out opportunities to sing in front of others, they will more than likely take action to avoid doing so.

Consider for a moment the huge solar panels that are used to track the sun to utilize solar energy. Wherever the sun moves in the sky, the solar panels follow its path in order to get maximum exposure.

Think of yourself like one of those solar panels. Your beliefs determine what your panels track. This is important. Your panels are programmed to track situations and experiences according to your beliefs. You will always get more of what you think about, because this is what you have programmed yourself to track. The stronger your belief, the more evidence you will accumulate to support your belief.

You track what you believe, regardless of whether your beliefs are true. If a person thinks they are a good singer, they will sing—even if they're actually appalling. Have you ever watched a talent show? Some people believe their talent to be greater than what others might perceive it to be. If there is enough feedback to the contrary, they may reevaluate and change their belief or get singing lessons and practice!

Vice versa, if you think you are a poor singer, you may have negative stories in your head with fears to support them—but you may actually be a good singer. Perhaps a jealous family member made unfortunate comments to you when you were young and impressionable, and you took on a negative belief that wasn't actually true.

Beliefs are just beliefs, and you can change them any time you wish. Just like software in your computer you, can delete old programs and install new ones. The computer has no option but to respond according to its programming—just like you.

If you want different results than the ones you are getting, you need to change your programming. Change your beliefs and change your life.

When you change your programming you change the experiences you track. Your solar panels will track whatever you program them for.

If your belief is that you are a fine-looking person, your panels will attract situations and people that will confirm your handsome appearance.

If you believe yourself to look ugly, your solar panels have no option but to track situations and people who will agree with you. You get more of what you think about.

This is why when you think negatively, things get worse. If you don't change your thinking, things get worse still. However, when you think positively, things continue to get better and better. They have no option. Hence, the more positive you are, the more positive situations you will attract. It's the law of attraction.

If you keep thinking the same things, you will keep getting the same results. If you want different results, it is essential to change your thinking. Unfortunately, some people not only don't realize this, but also take it a step further and try to get everyone else to change their thinking rather than doing their own inventory.

Be responsible for your own beliefs, thoughts, and actions rather than blaming your so-called bad luck on others or external circumstances. Your luck is ultimately determined by what you program your panels to attract.

When you change your beliefs, you change the perceptions people have of you. Your panels can only reflect messages that match.

The message or frequency you beam out to people is the one they receive. They have no option other than to receive what you send out. You determine what goes out—and by default, what comes back.

If you like the feedback people and your current experiences are giving you, then continue with what you are beaming out. *If you desire more positive experiences, beam out more positive messages.*

Television Set

Another way of understanding this is to think of yourself as the tuner on a television set. Your beliefs determine which channels you can tune in to—which stations you can pick up.

There's a myriad of signals or channels available, but if you believe yourself to be gorgeous, then the channel you'll be able to pick up is "channel gorgeous." This is the frequency you can receive. You will constantly tune in to "channel gorgeous." You will constantly see and hear "channel gorgeous," and this confirms and perpetuates your belief.

If your belief is that you're an excellent chef, you tune in to the frequencies or stations which support the belief that you are an excellent chef.

If you want particular experiences in your life, you need to tune in to the channels that present those experiences. For this, *you have to have the beliefs that allow you access to the channel.* You can only tune in to channels you have a subscription for.

You get to choose which channels or beliefs you subscribe to.

If you find yourself watching sports, and you love sports, that's great. If you're watching sports and you don't like sports, change channels. Change what you are subscribing to.

If your relationships aren't how you want them to be, change channels. Subscribe to good-relating channels.

If your finances aren't how you want them to be, change channels. Subscribe to wise-finance channels.

Choose which environment, health, appearance, work, and leisure channels suit you. It all starts with the beliefs you have about yourself. You alone choose these.

Match your beliefs, words, and actions to your purpose and the truth of who you are.

In order to heal, you need to know that you can.

In order to be calm, you need to believe yourself to be so.

To be slim and attractive, you need to believe this is normal for you. Release all doubt and sabotage. Know without a doubt that you are already healthy, and it is so. Know that you are calm, and it is so.

Be your own thought police. Every time you hear yourself say, "I am something," do a quick assessment and check if this is aligned with your purpose. Is it positive or negative? Does it match your intention? If it doesn't, then change it to something that does.

Control your mind.

Don't let the inmates run the asylum!

5. What's in Your Suitcase?

When you prepare to go on a journey, you take a number of things into consideration before you pack. Are you going to:

- A warm climate or cold?
- Another time zone or the same?
- Work or play?
- Another language?
- Similar or unfamiliar food?
- A comparable culture or different?
- A location that requires a passport or visa?

The more prepared you are for the journey, the better; however, even the best preparation doesn't always cover all contingencies.

Maybe you had planned appropriately for a warm climate, but the area had a cold snap. Or perhaps the food wasn't quite what you expected and left you unsettled. All manner of unexpected situations can pop up. That's life!

You usually need to make a choice when you need to adapt or change direction.

You can prepare for life with as much diligence as a backpacker choosing what to carry or leave behind; however, there are likely to be situations where an extra pair of clean socks would be appreciated.

If you plan to be a concert pianist, it makes sense to have an ear for music, fingers that can reach the keys, and the self-discipline to glue yourself to the piano stool to practice.

If you're going to be a landscape gardener, it would be appropriate to have a love for nature and plants, a knowledge for what grows where and how big, and the physical stamina to see projects through.

If you're going to be a university lecturer, it would fit to have a passion for learning and passing on knowledge. Some lecturers are more passionate than others, right?

Clearly, you are more than your body. When you leave your body at death, your body is still here. When you leave your body while you sleep, your body is still here.

Modern photographic techniques show that we are far more than our bodies. They can accurately demonstrate the aura and its fluctuations with sleep, attitude, health, and creed. They can show the contents of your suitcase—what you have packed.

What you have in your suitcase is only a fraction of what you have in your wardrobe—and indeed, your house. (You don't usually take your dining suite on your journeys, but leave it home for your return.) Likewise, what you have in your body is but a small part of you.

A suitcase has a limited size, so it makes sense to only take with you the items you are most likely to need. Likewise, your body has a limited healthy size, so you only pack into it what you consider you're most likely to need.

If you find you really could do with having your favorite chair—or more likely, your laptop—beach clothes, or a coat with you on your holiday, you can always send for it. You still have access to what you have at home. You just need retrieve and ship it.

If you find you really could do with some extra energy or wisdom, you can always send for it. You still have access to the greater parts of you that haven't been packed into your body. This is often referred to as your higher self.

If you are down in a valley, you can see as far as the landscape and your visual acuity permits. If you are up on a mountain, you can obviously see much further. From within your physical body, you have a certain ability to see; however, your higher self is on top of the mountain. It can see a bigger picture, and it can see further ahead.

It makes sense to stay in regular touch with your higher self! If you're away from home for an extended period, don't you stay in contact? If there are obstacles ahead, it's useful to be able to plan a solution. Is it best to go through, under, over, or around?

Grounding

Have you ever seen a tent blow away in the wind? The stronger the wind, the stronger, more deeply, and firmly planted into the ground the pegs need to be to avoid disaster.

Have you ever known anyone to go camping and not take the pegs at all? In this situation, even a slight breeze can play major havoc!

Sarah's Story

Whenever Sarah walked on a busy street, she would repeatedly have to duck and weave around other pedestrians. Whether the street was busy or not didn't seem to matter; she always had to dodge oncoming walkers. It always seemed like people were in her way.

Why was it that others could find a clear path through the crowd and walk without interruption, yet she was frustrated at the inconvenience of being constantly diverted to fit around others?

David's Story

David flew a lot with his work. Even though he took mostly short flights, he often found he wasn't fresh and ready to focus when he arrived. He also noticed that his body didn't stay firmly in his seat on landings. That is, when the plane was landing, his upper body would move forwards. Even though the plane was rapidly stopping, his body kept moving forwards.

Steve's Story

Steve was good at his work. He progressed well and was keen to learn. A large part of his job, however, involved gathering information from others. Sometimes he was right on the ball, and everything went smoothly—yet at other times, he would drift off in his own head and not even hear what people were saying to him. It's not that he wasn't interested, because he needed to know what they had to say, it's just that he didn't always take it in. Why was he so present sometimes and not at other times?

When you're ungrounded, you will have similar experiences to Sarah, David, and Steve. If you're ungrounded, you're the equivalent of a tent blowing around in the wind. This is not only frustrating, but also a waste of your time and energy, because you constantly have to make up for situations that didn't need to occur in the first place.

All three people solved their issues with ease simply by learning and applying grounding techniques, pegging their energy strongly and firmly into the earth every morning. Sara walked a clear path ahead without even thinking about it. David was able to think clearly and focus after flying. He could also sit firmly in his chair on landings. Steve was able to maintain his concentration and listen without forcing it.

It's also very common for people who are ungrounded to have great ideas but seem unable to put them into action. They either don't get started at all or get started and don't finish.

Exercise

Find a comfortable place where it's relatively quiet and you won't be interrupted for a few minutes. This exercise is easiest if you're standing up.

1. Close your eyes and take a gentle, easy breath in through your nose and out through your mouth. Keep breathing comfortably at your own pace.
2. With your next breath, take a breath in through your nose, and breathe out as if you're breathing down to your navel. Take a few breaths to practice. Even learning to walk took a bit of practice before you perfected it.
3. With your next breath, breathe in through your nose, and breathe out as if you're breathing down to your pubic bone. Take a few more breaths to get comfortable with this.

4. With your next breath, breathe in through your nose, and breathe out as if you're breathing down to your knees. Take a few more breaths.

5. With your next breath, breathe in through your nose, and breathe out as if you're breathing down to your feet. Take a few more breaths.

6. With your next breath, breathe in through your nose, and breathe out all the way to the core of the earth.

7. Mentally connect your energy to the core of the earth as if you're pegging your tent down. You actually have a main line of energy that travels through the top of your head, spine, and the lower half of your body. When you breathe in the above manner, you extend this main line of energy through to the core of the earth.

8. Breathe this earth energy from the core of the earth back up into your body. Breathe it into your heart.

This simple process grounds you. With practice, you'll be able to ground yourself in mere moments. You'll be able to breathe and send your energy all the way to the core of the earth without necessarily breathing to you navel, etc. first. Even so, it can really help you to relax if you breathe to the different parts of the body; don't dismiss something simply because you now find it easy.

If you're not certain of your direction in life, you will find that doing this simple grounding exercise each morning will help you get more clarity. It will help you get clear on your plans and have the stick-ability to follow them through. How good would it be to grow through your life, knowing your direction and having the persistence to follow it?

If you have children, wouldn't it be fantastic to teach them how to do this as well as incorporate it into your own daily routine? How good would it be to have a generation of grounded children growing through their lives, knowing their direction and having the persistence to follow it?

Connect to Your Source

Your body can't really be disconnected from your source without physically dying, because you are constantly connected by your silver cord. The lines of energy in the Master Diamond Blueprints for your body are silver, and the silver cord is an extension of these lines. It connects you like an umbilical cord to the creator, source, or universal intelligence. In truth, it's probably the other way around (i.e., *your Master Diamond Blueprint is an extension of the creator* connected by your silver cord).

Energy comes from above, down into your body, and then flows from the inside to the outside.

By reinforcing the connection to your source, you allow a smooth and continuous flow of universal energy into your physical and energy bodies. This will allow you continuous supply and save you from constantly using your own personal energy. Naturally, you will have more energy and be less tired.

Also, consciously connecting to your source allows you clearer access to your higher guidance. The more you establish the connection and keep your energy clean, the easier it will be to tune into the divine guidance from your higher self. This gives you clear access to all that is still in your wardrobe and house compared to what you packed in your suitcase.

By connecting to your source, you are connecting to your own philosophy, so it makes no difference what religion you do or don't have alignment with. You naturally connect to what you resonate with.

Exercise

This can be done as a natural continuation from your grounding exercise.

1. Put yourself in your quiet and comfortable space where you won't be interrupted.
2. After sending your grounding cords down into the earth by breathing your energy down through the soles of your feet and anchoring into the core of the earth, breathe in through your nose

and out through the top of your head. Take as many breaths as you need to get comfortable with this. Practice directing your breath until you master it easily. Don't give up on yourself, because clarity of purpose, more energy, confidence, and persistence can be your rewards.

3. Breathe up through the top of your head and extend your main line of energy all the way up to your source. Re-peg your energy into your source, the creator, God/Goddess, Universal Intelligence, or whichever label you're comfortable with.

4. Breathe Source's energy back down into your heart.

5. Continue the circuit, and breathe this source energy through the soles of your feet to the core of the earth and back up into your heart once more.

6. Feel your sense of stability, connection, clarity, and the extra energy you now have available to you. You are now connected to your higher self, Source, and the earth itself. It's a little like connecting to the internet. You now have access to far more than you do all by yourself!

7. Re-establish your connection every morning and whenever you want more clarity.

These grounding and connecting to Source exercises are simple and easy to do. You can do them virtually anywhere and anytime. You can also use the blend of 100 percent pure aromatherapy practitioner-grade oils which have been re-connected back to their source and botanical essences known as *Love Mist* or *Life Purpose Mist* to help you. Just spritz it over yourself each day. (See Appendix.)

6. It's Not What's Happening; It's How You Take It

Your body has an innate intelligence which:

- Knows to grow your fingers to the right length and stop—different lengths for different fingers, what's more!
- Converts the food you put in your mouth into muscles, organs, and bones.
- Keeps you breathing at the right rate and depth.
- Keeps your heart beating at the right rate and strength.
- Maintains your body temperature.
- Knows the difference between what's useful and what needs to be excreted as waste.
- Is connected to the intelligence of the universe and knows when you need to sleep, wake, find food, and prepare shelter.

This system is very fine-tuned; yet at a superficial glance, it could appear to have some faults. For instance, why do some people get sick while others don't? Why are some people fertile and others not? Why are some people compatible and others not?

When rivers travel down from the mountains, they encounter snags. The water can either go over the top of the snag or around it to continue its journey. It compensates or adapts.

When a tree grows, it extends its roots to maintain its balance and gather nutrients. If the roots encounter obstacles, they too have to compensate.

If a child has her feet bound tightly to prevent them from growing in their normal pattern, compensation occurs. They still grow, albeit in a different way than the original plan.

The same occurs when you incur emotional and mental challenges. When you are subjected to physical, emotional, or mental turmoil, you compensate. If there is a rock in your stream, you either find a way around it or get squashed against it. You adapt as best you know how, given your circumstances.

Generally speaking, you will adapt from either a place of love or fear. If you adapt from a place of love, you will gather up your strengths and resources and find the best possible solutions for yourself. Do you go over, under, around, or through?

If you adapt from a place of fear, you will often erode your hard work, self-esteem, and health. Getting angry at the rock, blaming someone for putting it there, or waiting for someone else to remove it are all fear-based and cause your energy to contract. When you react from fear, you diminish your ability to function as a positive and contributing person in your world. You are less likely to find the solution to your challenges, let alone have the confidence to follow them through if you make your choices from fear.

Making your choices from love and confidence expands your energy and expands your ability to see even more options and potential solutions.

Ellen's Story

Ellen was a traveler. She had a dream to travel and teach, to work in schools for a period of time and then move on to a new locations, students, and adventures. She wanted to make a difference.

She was blessed with meeting her soul mate and love of her life at an early age. He too was a traveler, and their plans fit like a glove.

Ellen discovered she was pregnant. Oh, what a blessing! But what about her travel plans? She was ready to explore the world with her mate! Instead, she relinquished her dream and stayed put.

She dutifully raised her child and even birthed another. It was a long journey, and the children grew into maturity and left home to follow their own innate paths. Still, Ellen stayed put. She had developed cancer and began another journey.

Andrea's Story

Andrea was a girl of purpose. From an early age, she wanted to make a difference in the world. She just needed to choose how. She studied the healing arts and established herself as a wonderful resource. She too became pregnant—not by the love of her life, but pregnant all the same. What about her career as a healer?

Andrea slowed down and took her baby to work with her. Patients waited while she breastfed and stayed to play as the little one grew. Was it Andrea's original plan? No, but she worked with what she had to make another plan that gave her the fulfillment she was looking for.

It's not what happens in your life that causes the problems, but how you respond to them. In every situation you find yourself in, there are always options.

It's well-known throughout history that many inmates of prisoner of war camps perished horribly; yet some inmates from the same circumstances survived. Some people survive the most obscene of atrocities, and a number of them go on to create much-needed social change in the world.

People think and act differently according to their beliefs and values. If you have something to live for—if you have a dream to fulfill—you can find a way. *If you focus on your blessings rather than your problems, your dreams can actually find a way to find you.* Focus past the problems and look for solutions. Energy comes from above, down, inside, and out. Allow the energy and the highest dreams of your pure essence to come in.

If you feed the weeds, they grow. If you focus on the problems, they have no choice but to get bigger.

Everyone has rocks on their course, and even though some may look smaller than others, a rock is a rock. With every encounter, you have the choice whether to look for solutions from a place of love (positive and expanding) or react from fear (negative and contracting).

If you focus on the rocks in the river and how much they are going to hurt when you hit them, you limit your ability to slide over or around them. Rocks are always going to be there. Don't blame the rocks! They are the blessings that make you find alternate ways of being. If it weren't for the rocks, you would have no reason to change—and without change, you don't grow.

That doesn't mean you should go searching for rocks. Head for the smooth part of the river, and go with the flow!

Just as some people behave as rocks for you, you too are a rock in other people's rivers. Others create challenges for you; you also create challenges for them. You attract the people and circumstances into your life that give you the opportunity to witness your behavior and beliefs and alter them accordingly. Your circumstances in life are mirroring your beliefs to you. They are showing what you hide from yourself.

It's not about getting anything right or wrong, as such. On the contrary it is a path to wholeness—a journey to oneness with many routes you can choose from to get there. The rocks are a gift. Be patient and forgiving with yourself as you enjoy your adventure.

When you are gentle with yourself, you will be more likely to be gentle with others as well. If you want others to be gentle with you, you also need to be gentle with both yourself and them.

The wars between nations are a reflection of wars inside us. The only difference between inner wars of low self-esteem and outer wars of lack of esteem for other people, countries, colors, or creeds is the magnitude and public consequence.

The war inside yourself kills and maims your cells, causing pain and disease—just as the outer wars kill and maim peoples and communities.

The pollution in your head from negative emotions, thoughts, and beliefs is reflected in the world as negative feelings, behaviors, and actions towards others. The toxicity in your body from additives, preservatives, colorings, flavorings, plastics, insecticides, herbicides, mould retardants, and the like have the same clogging and detrimental effects as the pollution we have created in the earth's air, waterways, and soil. As within, so without. What's on the inside eventually shows on the outside.

What you do in your life is what you create in your world. By responding to your challenges with a positive mindset and letting go of grudges, toxic emotions, thoughts, and beliefs, you have a chance of healing yourself and creating positive change in the world.

The outer world is important, but changing your inner world will bring lasting change into your life. It all starts on the inside. It all begins in your own heart. Go into the stillness of your heart and know your own truth. Make your choices from here.

7. Clean Yourself Up

As you go through your day, your physical body gets dirty, whether from your own perspiration and elimination of toxins and pollution in the air or handling dirty materials. Hence, you bathe or shower on a regular basis to keep yourself clean and smelling nice and to avoid creating a breeding ground for bacteria and inviting infection.

The electromagnetic field surrounding your body—also known as your aura, energy bodies, or Master Diamond Blueprints—also get dirty from the negative thoughts and emotions you create and from what you absorb from others. Just as it's essential to clean your physical body, it's also essential to clean your energy bodies—or else they become congested, trigger further negativity in you, and cannot function correctly.

The generalized cleaning of your energy bodies that remove the day-to-day energy grime you've accumulated is known as *clearing*. It is the equivalent of washing yourself. This is crucial if you want to have clear thinking, good health, and be able to function at peak potential. Clearing is the straightforward and indispensable daily wiping of the kitchen bench, rather than the meticulous scrubbing of the fridge or oven that's still to come.

It is essential to clean your energy daily and also take the time at regular intervals to do more multi-layered cleaning and removal of your deeper wounds.

All excess energy that doesn't serve you is negative to you. For example:

- Frustration
- Irritation
- Anger

- Fear
- Antagonism
- Apprehension
- Belligerence
- Jealousy
- Rage
- Bitterness
- Discontent

I could keep going, but I'm sure you get the idea.

Have you ever felt good and gone somewhere like a supermarket or bank and come away feeling irritable and exhausted? This is what happens when you absorb negative energy.

Places like supermarkets and banks are renowned for being full of negative energy. Customers are often in a rush, worried about money, and possibly even doing battle with noisy and uncooperative children. Children are also likely to be doing battle with uncooperative parents!

This is actually one of the reasons why sensitive children often behave so poorly in supermarkets. They absorb dirty energy and then react to it. The parents and other shoppers then tend to react to the child, and the cycle is perpetuated.

Bars are similar. Many people go there to drown their sorrows, only to leave their gripes behind for more sensitive people to absorb. Generally speaking, the busier the place, the more likely it is to have dirty energy; analogous to the fact that the busier the place, the more likely it is to get physically dirty. It makes sense, doesn't it?

On the other hand, quiet places in nature tend to be the opposite. They are generally more peaceful and have fresh air and trees to cleanse and transmute the stale energy. Be discerning, though, because cranky people can be cranky anywhere—in nature or not.

Has anyone ever dumped their problems on you?

If you have been in this position, you'll know exactly what I mean. Simply put, they shed their baggage, and you absorb it. There's no point getting upset and blaming them for dumping, because chances are, someone else dumped on them. And if you get upset at them, you're simply doing the same in return!

It's not a total solution to just remove yourself from being with others so you don't get dumped on, because then you miss out on all the good things, too. You need to be able to function in the world without fear and resentment.

Consistently look past problems and seek out solutions. Stay away from the chronic dumpers until you have fine-tuned your boundaries, cleared away the dross, and "protected" yourself regularly.

Energy is a two-way street. It's easy to see what other people do to us, but we can sometimes be blind to what we do to them. They, too, have to deal with the results of your negativity, frustration, confusion, anger, and resentment. Others affect you, and you affect others. Find your inner truth, live in peace—from a state of being rather than constantly doing—and be a positive influence.

As well as negative emotions, you can also absorb bad smells, heavy perfumes, loud sounds, and loud colors. Negative energy is negative energy, regardless of the source.

Even beautiful music can be negative if the volume is too loud or it's played on an instrument you don't like. Mismatched colors, designs, and textures can be like chalk on a blackboard to some. If you don't align with it, it's negative to you. That doesn't mean it's negative to everyone! Something you don't have an affinity with at all may resonate beautifully with someone else.

Have you ever felt:

- *Angry?* When you feel angry, you produce a lot of *red* energy in your energy field. Each color vibrates at a particular frequency, which is measurable. This is where the term "seeing red" comes from. Physically, red raises your heart rate and blood pressure, so it can be useful to use it to symbolize danger and to wear it for sports—but if you have a tendency toward anger, it's not a good idea to wear it, because it will add to your irritation.
  - Have you ever seen a hyperactive child eat red candy?
  - Have you ever tried to sleep on red sheets? They keep you active, not peaceful—which is fine, if your motive isn't to sleep!

- *So angry that you were furious?* When you feel rage, you produce a lot of *black* energy in your energy field. This is where the terms "black with rage" and "in a black mood" come from.
- *Sad?* When you feel sad, you produce a lot of *blue* energy in your energy field. This is where the phrase "got the blues" comes from. When you are feeling depressed, it's not a good idea to wear too much blue, because it will add to your blues.
- *Wishful that you had something another person had?* When you feel envious, you produce a lot of *green* energy in your energy field. This is where the term "green with envy" comes from. When you are feeling envious, it's not a good idea to wear too much green, because it will add to your jealousy.
- *You weren't up to a task?* When you feel apprehensive and lack confidence, you produce a lot of *yellow* energy in your energy field. This is where the term "yellow streak" comes from. When you're not feeling brave, it's not a good idea to wear too much yellow, because it will keep you in your head and can add to your thoughts of cowardice.

This doesn't mean these colors are bad. You can use a pen to write a beautiful love note or poke someone's eye out with it. Is the pen good or bad? Neither. It's what you do with it that counts! And it's the same with color. The color isn't good or bad; it's the intention behind it that matters. Plus, an overdose of anything can create problems.

For example:

- *Red* isn't good or bad; it's what you are doing with it that determines its effect on you. If you are cold and sluggish, red can raise your heart rate and blood pressure to get you up and running. It gets things moving. The problem is that when you are up and running in the wrong direction, it's not useful for you to run even harder and faster into more trouble. As always, balance and discernment are key.
- *Black* can hold your energy within and shut you down. You probably don't want this when you are with your family and friends; however, this might be useful if you don't want to share yourself in large crowds of assorted people and attitudes.

- *Blue* can slow you down. It can lower your heart rate, lower your blood pressure, calm you when you are stressed, and cool you when you are hot.
- *Green* can be very soothing and harmonizing. Remember how calming it feels like to walk through a lovely, green garden? Green is the spectrum of energy that protects you from the effects of other people's emotions.
- *Yellow* can stimulate your mind and intellect. It can help your thought process, help your memory, help you to learn, and also help you recall what you have learnt.

The colors themselves are not good or bad; it's your intent that determines their effect.

Every time you have a negative intent, you will create a negative effect. Every time you have a positive intention, you will create a positive effect.

Multiple emotions naturally create multiple colors in your energy field. This creates murky brown or grey energy, and this is not what you want overriding the pristine balance of your energy bodies. It ends up like the mess of mixed colors in a child's paint pot—everything goes grey, and you lose the definition of the beautiful colors underneath.

All dirty energies around you interfere with your true expression and health and need to be cleared as soon after they've been created as possible. They interfere with the signal to your television set and make it hard for you to tune in to any worthwhile station. It is far better if we don't create or allow ourselves to absorb negative energies that aren't aligned with the higher expression of ourselves in the first place; however, we are human!

Symptoms—how do you know if you need clearing?

It's ideal to clean your physical body every day by showering or bathing—even more so if you do things in the day that warrant it (such as after sports, gardening, doing dirty or contaminated work, or even washing your hands after using the bathroom).

Likewise, it's ideal to clean your energy bodies every day—even more so if you do things that warrant it (such as feeling irritated, angry, fearful, worried, stressed, antagonized, apprehensive, jealous, bitter, discontented, or being around others who are). There are some extra clues that will tell you when you specifically need clearing.

Negative energies can make you feel anything from mild annoyance to irrational temper. When you feel annoyed or express your temper when there's been nothing worthy of triggering it, you have negative energies affecting you.

When the negative energies are extreme, they can cause you to feel nausea and even vomit. If you feel nausea or are vomiting and there's been no bad smells or bad food worthy of triggering it, you have a high density of negative energy affecting you.

It's important to notice if you are feeling annoyed about things that wouldn't normally bother you or you're feeling nauseous and you haven't eaten or smelt anything that would warrant it, because it not only affects your own behavior and health, but also affects everyone around you who you dump on when you're like this.

How to Clear Yourself

There are a number of ways to clear yourself, so try them all and see which gives you the best results. Many people prefer to combine a couple of different ways at the same time. I think of it a bit like detergents—some are better than others, depending what's going on. Dish detergent may be great for your glassware, but not so effective for cleaning the oven.

It's a good baseline routine to clean your energy every morning and night—just like you clean your teeth.

Visualization

Simply visualize the negative energies as murky energy surrounding your body and mentally wash it up to the universal white light above your head. It is important to send it up to the light (actually picture it binding to the light), because if you just remove it from yourself and leave it hanging around, you or someone else will just pick it up again. Think of it like a spilt drink in space. It doesn't just go away. It floats around until something else takes it up.

Affirmation

You can focus your positive words with intention to remove negative energy. The more you focus, the better the result. Affirm or state with intention something like:

- "I bind all negatives within and surrounding my aura up to the white light for transmutation into positivity."
- "I now clear everything negative affecting myself, raise it up, and bind it to the light."
- "I clear all energies that do not resonate 100 percent with me."
- Recite "The Lord's Prayer" if you feel comfortable with it. Within Christianity, the Lord's Prayer has been used for centuries to shift negativity. Saying "Amen" at its completion seals your chakras or energy centres. If you're aligned with another religion, simply chant the equivalent cleansing and protecting prayer of your faith.

Use affirmations that suit you and clearly state your intention to cleanse yourself of negative energies, and bind them so you or anyone else doesn't reabsorb them.

Color

Different colors do different things. *Amber is the color that clears negative energy.* It is also known as the color of first aid, largely because of its usefulness in helping fight infections.

If you can arrange a forty-watt amber globe above the doorway to your house and office, it will clear the negative energies of the people as they enter. The less negativity comes into your space, the better. The globe needs to be forty-watt or less, or else the color will be dispersed too much to be effective.

Chakra Clearing Meditation

You can do focused meditations to clear your energy field—specifically, its energy centres or chakras. Focus on cleaning your entire energy field of all:

- Negative thoughts
- Negative emotions
- Negative beliefs
- Limiting beliefs

If you need assistance to commit to your daily clearing practice, you can use the *Be In One Peace™* Chakra Clearing Meditation CD to guide you through the necessary steps.

Aromatherapy

Peace Mist is a blend of 100 percent pure aromatherapy practitioner-grade oils which have been connected back to their source and botanical essences. Just spritz it over yourself each morning, night, and whenever you need to clear yourself. It removes the dirty and dense energies you encounter every day—whether from your own frustration and tension or from others' dramas. You can also use it to rid your mind of unwanted thoughts and negative self-talk and dissolve the vines of restriction. (See Appendix.)

Peace Mist is also excellent to clear rooms at home and in workplaces by spraying into the four corners as well as generously into the centre of the room. If necessary, spray all exits such as doors, windows and ventilation shafts.

Body Washes

Use can use *Aura Cleanser Body Washes* in your bath or shower daily to clean your physical body and aura simultaneously. They have no animal content, no artificial colors, no artificial fragrances, are not tested on animals, are eco-friendly, and are in recyclable containers.

They are blends of 100 percent aromatherapy practitioner-grade pure essential oils, Cordyline terminalis and Acorn botanical essences, and Amethyst vibrational essence in a sodium lauryl sulphate-free liquid soap.

If your energy is particularly congested or blocked, use an aura cleanser on a loofah for deeper cleansing. It's revitalizing!

Botanical Essences

Angelsword is an Australian Bush Flower Essence that helps remove negative energies from your aura. It is a botanical essence which comes in a dropper bottle. The standard dose is seven drops under your tongue each morning and night for two weeks.

The Three-Candle Burning Method

This is one of the most powerful methods for clearing negative energy, hence, it's one of my favorites! It's not always practical, depending on your circumstances; however, it's very efficient.

Just as fire clears out the dead wood in a forest, you can use it to clear out dead or negative energy. You need:

- Three white or beeswax candles. Say a dedication or blessing over the candles to dedicate them to the white light of positivity (e.g., you can leave them in a holy book such as the Bible or your equivalent overnight). Then say a dedication (such as the Lord's Prayer or your equivalent) to align them with the light.
- Three *non-metal* candle holders.
- A heatproof non-metal dish. (Metal binds the negativity to you— the exact opposite of what you want!) A ceramic breakfast bowl is okay however purpose made "Burning Dishes" with built in candle holders are available.
- White porous paper. (It burns easily without smoking you out!)

1. *Write appropriate clearing words that contain all the necessary information for clearing negative energies on the paper.* For example, say "I now burn and clear everything negative including pass-overs and step-out step-ins affecting [insert the person or people's names/the address], raise it up and bind it to the light in the name of [insert whatever represents "good" to you, e.g., the Lord Jesus Christ/Lord Buddha/Universal Intelligence/God/Goddess]. (See Glossary for more information on earthbound souls and step-out step-ins.)

2. Write the three symbols of protection on the bottom of the paper—the symbols for protection and infinity and the balanced cross: Y   ∞   ✚

3. Fold the paper in half and then in half again so the creases form a cross. This also represents the four elements: earth, air, fire, and water.

4. Light the three dedicated candles arranged symmetrically in a triangle around the heatproof bowl. Ignite your folded piece of paper with your clearing words on it, from each of the three of candles, and *make certain that all of the paper burns.* You may need to poke it with a wooden match or skewer (non-metal) or drip wax on it to ensure that it burns completely.

Once you are well practised with your candles, you can create your own symbol to burn for the things that you regularly clear. You may create a symbol for clearing your immediate family, your house, your workplace or work mates, etc. Do them one at a time on separate pieces of paper. Write your clearing words and symbols followed by "this equation now equals [add your own symbol]," fold your paper twice, and burn this. From then on, you only need to write your own symbol on twice-folded paper and burn it. It's a good idea to establish the energy and your intent by completing the full procedure for some weeks before you take shortcuts. To get good results, you need a strong, focussed, and established energy.

Use any of these methods individually or in combination. Find what suits you best and clear yourself and your immediate environment every day.

How to Clear Your Environment
Aromatherapy

- *Peace Mist* Spray into the four corners as well as generously into the centre of the room. If necessary, spray all exits such as doors, windows, and ventilation shafts.
- *Musk incense* Burn musk incense generously and regularly. Incense on its own without the focus of pure thought and intention is generally not strong enough to shift dense negativity. Like detergent for cleaning glassware, it's not strong enough to "clean the oven."
- *Smudge stick* Burning smudge sticks of dried sage leaves or blends of sage, rosemary, and other herbs is a traditional American Indian method of cleansing an environment. You can also waft smudge sticks over yourself for cleansing. Some people love the smell of burning sage, and others find it offensive. I suggest you use the methods you like. Australian Aboriginals burn eucalyptus leaves for the same result.

Visualization

Visualize a tornado of white light going through all the rooms and sending all negative energy up to the white light. Then mentally fill the room or rooms you have cleared with white light. White light is pure energy. When you have removed the dross, replace it with the positivity of white.

Color

As previously mentioned, keep a forty-watt, amber-colored globe alight above your front door to clear negative energies from people before they enter your home or workplace. Amber is the color which clears negativity.

8. Protect Your Assets

It's easy to absorb unwanted energies and end up feeling deflated, tired and irritable. Since you're subject to everyone's emotions on a daily basis, its better you follow the adage that "prevention is better than cure" and protect yourself so you aren't so permeable to negative influences.

When you've cleared yourself, you've removed the dirty energy that was there—but this doesn't stop you from either absorbing or creating more. You are open to picking up whatever energy people are spraying around—unless you take steps to protect yourself from it.

Just as you wear clothes to protect yourself from the physical environment—the sun, wind, cold, and the long arm of the law—it is essential to put on your energetic clothes to protect yourself from the energetic environment.

It is essential to keep yourself protected from energetic pollution all day, every day—not just every now and then or when you get so exhausted and desperate you finally think of it! The modern world bombards you with constant input: traffic and industrial noise, advertising, television, radio, iPods, computers, signs, billboards, e-mail, internet, phones, electromagnetic radiation, electricity, high-voltage power lines, ultrasound, X-rays, opinions, emotions, and tantrums. Your eyes, ears, and nose are particularly bombarded with stimuli. Even when you're asleep, you're within the energy field of your partner, who hasn't necessarily had a peaceful day or been around others who have.

In the past, it was generally considered that energetically or psychically protecting yourself morning and night was enough. However, in the past, there wasn't the constant barrage that you are subjected to now. It may be necessary to clear and protect yourself even more regularly. Mentally surround yourself with strong, pure, white energy at regular intervals throughout your day. It's more essential than ever to look after yourself and maintain healthy boundaries for yourself. This simply requires attention and focus.

Energetic protection and psychic protection are often used interchangeably. They are simply referring to guarding yourself from absorbing aberrant energies and frequencies that don't sustain you.

Anger disperses your protection. Every time you feel angry or you're around someone else who is angry, you'll need to clear yourself again and replace your white light protection.

If you suppress anger instead of expressing it, you will store it in your body. Anger particularly affects your liver, and if this vital organ becomes congested, a myriad of biochemical functions gets interrupted. Your liver directly influences your hormones, blood sugar, energy levels, detoxification processes, and digestion. If it becomes overloaded, you can feel physically and emotionally depressed, irritable, angry, tired, and generally unwell. Also, anger stores in your thighs; hence the term "thunder thighs." Large thighs are not a result of bad luck or bad genes; they are from unresolved anger.

At first, you may not recognize how often you feel angry, but even when you experience situations such as feeling the annoyance of someone cutting you off in traffic or people keeping you waiting with no respect for your time, these are symptoms of anger.

Initially, you may find that clearing and protecting is a full-time job. However, the more diligent you are, the less you'll feel angry in the first place, because your energy will become consistently cleaner over time. The cleaner your energy, the easier it is for you to choose how to respond to people and situations rather than react. This in itself helps prevent the formation of negative energy at the cause.

The more tuned in you become, the more you'll be aware how much fear and anger reign in our current world. If you're not protecting yourself from this, there's a high chance you'll absorb it and hence suffer the consequences. Unfortunately, you're then likely to be just as human as everyone else and perpetuate the cycle with others.

If you're not as meticulous with clearing and protection as necessary, you'll feel tired, irritable, and possibly over-sensitive. In the extreme, you'll feel nauseous for no apparent reason. Use these as indicators to do extra clearing and protection on top of your morning and night routine.

As a parent, you have the responsibility to look after your children as best you know how; this includes keeping them energetically safe with clearing and protection. Parents are legally responsible for the guardianship of their children until they become adults. This age varies from country to country. Clear and protect them each morning and night as you do yourself until they're responsible enough to do it for themselves.

Isabella's Story

Isabella was a regular teenager who loved to go to concerts. She headed off with her friends to have a good time, but always came home exhausted, irritable, and often vomiting. At first it was thought that she had eaten something foxy—but even when she didn't eat at all, she would come home affected.

Her energy was wide open in anticipation of a great night out and absorbed every bit of rubbish energy around her. By learning to protect herself before she went out, Isabella was able to enjoy the music without paying the price of being the energetic sponge. Clearing away the dross left her ready and able to function normally again. (This was prior to concerts being synonymous with illicit drug use.)

In our modern times, younger and younger people are attending large concerts where the energy is high—and more often than not, so are the people. Mind-altering drugs are one of the biggest culprits for putting holes in people's auras and their natural energetic shields. This is why many people who get into drugs find they can't stop even after minimal exposure. The drugs put holes in the aura so the person doesn't feel good, so then they want more drugs until they get to where they feel dependant. Sadly, the continued use creates even more holes, and the problem worsens. With particularly sensitive individuals, they don't even need to take the drugs themselves. If they are around others who are smoking mind-altering substances, they can be affected just by breathing the expelled air of others.

How Can You Protect Your Energy Field?

There are a variety of ways you can protect yourself. This is largely because we are all different, and we're also exposed to a wide variety of people and energies. If everything and everyone was the same, we might only need one way. Whichever way you choose, make sure you clear the negative energy away before you use your protection, or else it's a bit like washing the floor before you sweep it. If you protect yourself before you clear yourself and you have an earthbound soul attached to you, you're also protecting that soul rather than sending it on to the light to continue its journey.

White Light

White light has all the colors of the spectrum within it—red, orange, yellow, green, blue, indigo, and violet. It is often referred to as the Universal White Light of Protection.

When you mentally surround yourself with white light, this is traditionally referred to as "putting on your robe of white light."

See in your mind's eye a bright, white light above your head. Shine it so it totally encompasses you, including underneath your feet. Picture this as if you're the star on a stage with the spotlight of white light totally surrounding you.

The stronger your focus, the stronger your protection will be, and the longer it will last.

Affirmation

There's power in words. Use your words and affirmations to create what you choose. Use your words and phrases with focus and intention. Choose words you're comfortable with, and state your intention clearly. The more you affirm your words, the faster and stronger you will feel the effects of them. You can create your own affirmation or use tried and true ones that others have used through history.

For example:
• "I cover myself in a beautiful robe of white light" (Chira).

• "I clothe myself in a robe of white light composed of the love, power, and wisdom of God—not only for my own protection, but also that all who see it and come in contact with it are drawn to God and healed" (Isabel Hickey).

Silver Bubble

A silver bubble of energy is best used around the outside of your white light as an added protective shell. Picture white light around yourself first; *then* put a silver bubble around the perimeter for added strength. The silver bubble reflects aberrant energies that are headed your way and also helps stop your white light from dissipating.

Aromatherapy

• *Peace Mist.* Use it generously as a personal spray and room spray to help protect from negativity. When you use it regularly, you clear negative energies from you and your surroundings. It also provides an effective defense against negative energies directed at you. The advantage Peace Mist has over the other methods of clearing and protection is that it does both—it both clears and protects.
• *Sandalwood.* Use 100 percent pure Sandalwood essential oil in conjunction with your visualization and affirmation techniques.
   ▪ Put approximately seven drops of pure essential oil in an oil burner or oil diffuser (depending on the size of the room). Be aware that Sandalwood has a reputation as an aphrodisiac, so you may find yourself surrounded by people who feel happier—but for different reasons!
   ▪ In some eastern traditions, a daily drop of sandalwood is used on the third eye and nape of the neck for protection.

100 percent pure sandalwood essential oil is usually expensive. Make certain you get what you're paying for. If it's cheap, it may be a fragrance oil (manufactured to simulate an essential oil but

doesn't contain all the qualities) diluted in carrier oil or cut with less expensive ingredients.

Botanical Essences

• *Fringed Violet* is an Australian Bush Flower Essence which repairs holes in your aura and makes it less permeable to outside energies. The standard dose is seven drops under your tongue each morning and night for two weeks, and then again as required.

~~~

Use any or all of the above methods. Find what is the most effective for you. By clearing and protecting yourself regularly, your mood will be better, your decision-making will be clearer, and you'll find it easier to maintain your personal boundaries.

9. Remove Your Armor

People spend too much time and energy fitting in with other people, compromising their beliefs and principles, and selling themselves short.

If you think you're tired of being you, then you might actually be tired of not being you. Many of your problems in life are a result of not being true to yourself.

Every time you sell yourself short—even if it is dressing a certain way so you'll fit in rather than wearing what you really want or eating what everyone else is eating when you really want something else—you add a layer of armor over yourself.

Persona comes from Latin and means "mask." It is the social role or character we learn to play. You acquire elements throughout your life and blend them together to continually modify your persona, or mask. Year after year of adding layers leaves you with a protective coating like armor. Even though these layers were added with the good intention of keeping you safe, what you need to keep you safe as a child is often no longer relevant as an adult.

Baby elephants at the circus are chained to a strong pole in the ground to make sure they don't run off. As strong as they are, they can't pull the pole out of the ground or break the chain and free themselves. Adult elephants are tethered relatively flimsily. They were trained as babies to think they can't break free, so they stop trying!

What are the layers of armor you acquire to keep you safe? Maybe you played the good girl or boy with your parents to stay out of trouble. Maybe you played the bad girl or boy to stay in synch with your friends. Maybe you learnt to use humor or sarcasm to deflect hurtful remarks—or perhaps to physically fight. Did you learn to verbally or physically attack prior to potential pain—to inflict it to avoid receiving it? Or was it something else for you? All the tactics you have layered on yourself have been a means to an end. Unfortunately, though, they mask the real you.

This armor may have been essential to defend yourself as a child, but it only serves to keep the true essence of you buried. If the reason for the armor is no longer present, then you no longer need the armor. Even if it was humor you developed as a defense, it can stop you from feeling your deepest feelings by keeping your interactions at a superficial level.

Intimacy means "into me see." If you don't allow people to see into you, you will never have true intimacy.

The more you peel back the layers and allow the real you to emerge, the more you will be aligned with your soul and divine purpose and ultimately feel fulfilled. You cannot feel fulfilled when you no longer know who you really are—when you don't know who you "be."

Every time you wear a mask, you add to your armor and the false image you project. It also takes extra energy from your energy budget to maintain the armor. It can be perpetuated by such things as:

Food

Are you eating:

- What is convenient?
- What suits someone else?
- What you've been programmed to eat in the past rather than what you know your body needs for optimum function right now?

Remind yourself to be true to you instead of fitting in with whatever others are eating.

Clothes

Are you:

- Wearing styles, colors, or fabrics that aren't your preference?
- Influenced by fashion rather than your own personal style?

- Wearing hand-me-downs you don't like?
- Wearing the same old styles out of habit?
- Avoiding updating because of poverty consciousness (i.e., thinking you can't afford it and wearing something else)?
- Wearing a uniform that doesn't suit you? In many jobs, wearing a uniform is a condition of employment. If you can, wear undergarments in colors and styles that appropriately reflect you, and change into your own clothes as soon as you get home.

Music

Are you:

- Listening to music you don't like? This is a common issue in shared households—especially when different generations are involved! It may help to remember your music might be just as disturbing to others as theirs can be to you.

Behavior

Are you:

- Restricting your behavior to make someone else happy? This is sure to add layers on your armor!
- Behaving a certain way to make someone else unhappy? You might be surprised how many people actively seek revenge!

Principles and Beliefs

Are your principles and beliefs a reflection of what you really consider to be truth, or are they an inherited template from others?

- Do you vote for politicians you choose or in accordance with influential people around you?
- Do you not vote in accordance with people around you?
- Do you purchase products you really like, or the same ones your family or friends buy?

- Do you watch the programs and movies you want, or do you fit in with what other people choose?
- Do you follow the same religion as that of the family you were born into, or have you investigated others to consciously choose for yourself?

I'm not suggesting that everyone else's influence is not good for you. Simply be discerning about what is true for you, what isn't, and act accordingly.

Occupation

Are you:

- In your occupation because you love it, or did someone else steer you in that direction against your true desire?
- Doing it for the money?
- In an occupation where armor is a pre-requisite? Do you have a script you have to follow or formula you have to adhere to as part of the presentation you are required to make for your job? If this is the case, it is essential for you to take off this mask when you finish work each day—or if it really doesn't suit you, find a new job—or else you risk losing your real self in the persona of the job.

The more layers of armor you surround yourself with, the more you will feel the need to defend yourself.

Vice versa, the more you defend yourself, the more layers of armor you are surrounding yourself with.

Your armor serves a purpose. It keeps things out. But it keeps everything out—not just the things you feel the need to defend yourself from. If you're not careful, you can acquire so many layers of masking you forget who you really are. One of the clues this may be happening is when other people think you are something that you know you're not. If people don't know the real you, then you have been hiding it from them! They can only pick up the impressions you give them. If you project anything other than your true self, people will misinterpret who you are.

Removing layers of your false persona can sometimes make you feel a little vulnerable. After all, this is why you put the layers of protection there to begin with—to hide where you were feeling exposed and at risk. Vulnerability is a small price to pay—many successful people see it as an asset for the reward of freeing yourself from the shackles of your past and discovering who you really are.

If you leave the layers in place, the real you stays buried and lost, and you'll continue having to compromise and defend yourself. The more you do this, the more out of balance you and your life become. Alternately, you can shed your mask and revel in the freedom and confidence that's previously escaped you.

Have the courage to remove your defensive shields of armor and allow the world to benefit from the genuine you. You are a child of God and have a lot to offer. Allow yourself to feel fulfilled. Indulge in the rewards of health, love, and a sense of belonging.

I have regularly guided people in meditation to remove their armor and been amazed at the response from such a simple exercise. They regularly report amazing experiences ranging from releasing old emotions and un-forgiveness of people and situations to rushes of self-confidence and self-esteem they hadn't realized prior. The results often far exceed expectations.

Exercise

1. Sit in your quiet and comfortable space, where you won't be disturbed.
2. Mentally clear all negative energies from you, bind them to the white light, and protect yourself by surrounding your entirety with white light.
3. Relax and close your eyes.
4. Picture a receptacle in front of you to hold the armor you're shedding. If you have trouble visualizing, physically put something like a box in front of you. Do whatever you need to make it easy for yourself!
5. Gently close your eyes and relax.

6. Mentally take off your gloves and place them in the receptacle/box in front of you. Take a breath in. Breathe out and release.

7. Take off your sleeves and place them in the receptacle. Take a breath in. Breathe out and release. Take as much time as you need.

8. Remove your helmet and place it in the receptacle. Take a breath in. Breathe out and release. Keep breathing at your own comfortable pace.

9. Remove your boots and liners and put them in the receptacle. Take a breath in. Breathe out and release.

10. Remove your leggings and put them in the receptacle. Take a breath in. Breathe out and release.

11. And lastly, remove your chest plates, and put them in the receptacle. Take a breath in. Breathe out and release.

12. If there is anything else you wish to release, then shed it, too, and place it in the receptacle. Take a breath in. Breathe out and release.

13. Sit quietly and peacefully, breathing at your own pace, and *give thanks for all the protection the armor has provided. Acknowledge that it has served its purpose and that you no longer need it.*

14. Mentally send the receptacle and all its contents up to the universal white light for transformation. (If you used a physical bucket, send all the contents up to the light and perhaps clean your bucket with salty water.)

15. Ask that you be refilled with pure, white light. When you remove energy, you need to replace it with positivity, or else you leave a space where old habits can return.

16. Ask that all your energy bodies be energized, aligned, and sealed so you don't leak the energy you have replenished yourself with.

17. Re-establish your grounding cord. Breathe in through your heart, breathe down through your feet, extend your main line of energy, and connect it to the core of the earth

18. When you're ready, wriggle your toes and fingers and open your eyes.

You may feel like you need a glass of water or feel the need to write down any blinding flashes of discovery after this exercise. Many people feel the need to be quiet and like to indulge in their newfound self. This is the real you that has always been there ;it's just that you have rediscovered it. Honor yourself in a way that feels best for you. Enjoy what emerges and unfolds for you. Think of yourself as a pupa emerging from its cocoon and transforming into a beautiful butterfly. Allow yourself to fly!

10. Energy Budget

One of the most common complaints I hear in my practice is tiredness. Exhaustion and fatigue have become epidemic in modern society.

When you're doing more than usual you might expect to get tired, but when you are doing the same things you always do and you're getting tired, then something is wrong. Consider that maybe you've always been overdoing it!

If you do too much without adequate compensation—such as nutritious food, clean water, rest, meditation, or sleep—your body will remind you to pay attention—usually through pain, clumsiness, or accidents. Tiredness and illness are your body's way of getting your attention so you will change what you are doing.

When you're inappropriately tired, something is wrong. The most obvious cause of this is *too much energy out and not enough energy in,* which are perpetuated by:

- Faulty nutrition
- Faulty assimilation
- Overexertion
- Not enough recuperation and replenishment
- Energy drains
- A combination of the above

When you are tired, there is a tendency to crave sugar, because it is an easily absorbed and readily available energy. It is a quick fix. In the short term, this may be deceptively helpful to give you temporary energy to complete a task; however, it's a "band-aid" fix, wears off, and can set up a negative spiral of wanting more and more sugar. The problem escalates when your give in to the cravings and the quick fix becomes a regular occurrence or habit.

When you use sugar to supply your energy instead of budgeting your energy expenditure more wisely, you end up energy bankrupt.

This exhausts your adrenal glands and can cause problems, such as:

- Hormone imbalance
- Poor eyesight
- Tired legs
- Food sensitivities
- Cellulite
- Mood swings
- Blood pressure changes
- Skin problems
- Bacteria and yeast overgrowth

This can set you up as a candidate for diabetes, Candida infestation, and chronic fatigue syndrome.

Natural Ways to Restore Your Energy

It is far more sustaining to replenish your energy in ways that support it rather than just giving it more sugar and whipping it to continue a high output.

These include:

- Resting
- Sleeping
- Eating quality foods
- Spending time in nature
- Meditation

Even so, it's best to not become energy bankrupt in the first place!

Overeating to build up your energy is erroneous, because the consequences of an overburdened digestive system and excess weight will just add to your woes. Besides having to lug around the extra bulk, fat cells produce estrogen, which can create or exaggerate imbalances in your hormone system.

Every day, you allocate your energy according to the functions you need to perform. You give a percentage of your energy to:

- Digestion
- Thinking
- Breathing
- Hearing
- Seeing
- Working
- Movement

When you give more energy to an area than your budget allows, you either have to take more energy in or borrow some from another area. When you borrow from another area, it too becomes depleted, and then further problems will soon follow.

Worry and resentment are two of the biggest consumers of your energy. *Where your mind goes, the energy flows.* Your energy goes to what you think about. If you are worrying about something or someone or reliving in your mind some past event, your energy is going to this and feeding it.

Likewise, if you project your energy into the future and potential situations, this too will consume your energy. Whatever you think about consumes your energy budget and gets bigger. The more you resent something or someone, the more you perpetuate the issue.

Resentment is merely "re-sending" or re-thinking about something or someone. Perhaps you do it more than you think. *Remind yourself to live in the present.* The present is the gift, remember.

When you think about people and situations, you actually send cords of your energy out to them. If you don't cut these cords, your energy will whittle away, even though you've gone on to focus on other things.

This can leave you feeling tired even when you have had plenty of sleep, hungry even when you have had plenty to eat, and even give you a nuisance cough when you don't have a cold.

People who get a bloody nose for no apparent reason are often extreme in pouring their energy out to someone or something. These people are often exhausted.

Energy cords or drains often come from your abdominal region, because this is our feeling centre. When these cords or drains are active, they can pull your abdomen forwards and distend it, giving you a "Buddha belly." This distension can upset your digestion and contribute to Candida overgrowth and food sensitivities. The cords of energy we give out to people tend to come from our feeling centre or solar plexus. The cords we feed to times, places, situations, and events tend to come from the outer perimeter of the feeling centre diamond. The lines of energy in our Master Diamond Blueprints are very structured and geometrical; hence, different frequencies of energy naturally have an affinity with different regions.

The pulling forwards from these cords and the distension of your abdomen can also cause you to have a sway back. This is an added disaster if you wear high heels, because the shoe height forces your body into a position of compensation, which then exaggerates your sway back even further.

Add a pregnancy to this, and the spinal compensation escalates even further!

This is of major importance. It's not just about body shape! The nerves that exit your lumbar spine where the sway back is control all the organs in your pelvis, including reproductive organs, bladder, and bowels. When your spine is distorted, the nerve messages also get distorted, and malfunction of the organs and associated muscles result.

Do you:

- Have a sway back?
- Have a tummy that is flat or protruding?
- Experience gas?
- Have food sensitivities?

Can you see how important it is to manage your energy?

Signs that You Have Energy Drains or Cords

The more of these symptoms you have and the more severe they are, the longer or higher you're likely to have been allowing yourself to be drained. In truth, we actually give our energy away because no-one can take it without our permission on some level.

Watch for these clues:

- Tiredness, fatigue, or exhaustion
- Distended abdomen
- Digestive problems or food sensitivities
- Candida overgrowth or thrush
- Craving for carbohydrates
- Flatulence
- Plenty to eat and inability to stop
- Plenty of sleep and tiredness
- Sway back or lumbar hyperlordosis
- A nuisance cough when you don't have a cold
- Bloody noses for no apparent reason

Re-balance Your Energy Budget

No one can take your energy without your permission. If you are giving out too much or allowing your energy to whittle away, then it is up to you to:

- Set appropriate personal boundaries and maintain them
- Unplug from who and what you are frittering away your energy on
- Use your energy wisely

Only think about what you want, and don't give energy or power to the things you don't want. Your energy goes to what you think about, so make sure you are feeding the things you want and not the people and situations that are an unnecessary drain on you.

Call your energy back in from all the people, situations, times, places, and events into which you have invested it. You can do this mentally. The stronger your focus and intention, the better your results will be.

Exercise

Focus on the energetic cords that emanate from your abdomen and solar plexus regions—even if you can't see them.

1. Visualize each cord and mentally put two clamps or tourniquets on each—i.e., seal the two sections of the cord so when you cut them, they won't leak.
2. Mentally cut in between the two clamps—i.e., sever the cords that have been draining you.
3. Keep clamping and cutting until you have removed all the cords.

If you are connected to someone and they are connected to ten or twenty other people, then you too are connected to all the people they are giving their energy to. Your energy is going to them as well as the original person. Is it any wonder you get tired?

It is essential to cut off the cords you give out every night before you go to sleep—otherwise your energy will still be depleting overnight rather than replenishing, and you will wake up just as tired as when you went to bed—if not even more so!

This is particularly important if you share your bed, because your energy physically overlaps with your partner's, and your energy can go to the other person as you sleep. This can still happen over distance, but it is even more pronounced when you are in close physical proximity.

Effective products which can assist you in cutting cords are:

- *Angelsword* is an Australian Bush Flower Essence which effectively cuts off cords you give out to people. Simply put a drop on your solar plexus regularly. If you are a chronic giver, use a squirt rather than just a drop! Angelsword doesn't prevent you from creating the cord in the first place, but it will help you sever it. It's up to you to stop reinstating the cord and giving your energy away.

- *Dirogenia* is from the Essences of the Ancient Civilizations range. This cuts off cords to situations or events. It is best if you spread the drop around the outside of the feeling centre diamond (the diamond-shaped blueprint of the solar plexus).

Laura's Story

Laura lived on the west coast and had struggled with her weight for a number of years. She was active and watched what she ate but always seemed to have a "healthy appetite."

Her daughter, Sue, lived on the east coast and had been having marital problems since her marriage's inception. After many years of persistent difficulty and compromise, Sue finally divorced and moved on.

Miraculously, Laura lost five kilograms (eleven pounds) in three weeks, doing nothing obviously different! Without realizing it, she had been feeding her daughter energy while her daughter had been having difficulties, and she had been eating to compensate for it. Once the emotional upheaval was over, so too was the need for extra energy. Laura no longer had to eat extra to keep up her supply.

Laura had no conscious knowledge she had been energetically feeding Sue, and Sue had no conscious knowledge she had been draining her mother.

11. Group Over-Souls

An over-soul is the universal mind, spirit, or energy that animates, motivates, and unifies a given group or family. Every group you currently contribute to—and every group you have previously contributed to—has an over-soul, much like every child has a family. Even if you no longer have anything to do with your family or even remember who they are, you are still an energetic member of the group.

This connection between people has been demonstrated many times with the uncanny connection and communication between twins. This same connection is present for everyone—it's just been more pronounced or obvious with twins until now. As people awaken to their potential and have more awareness of their interconnection with everyone and everything, they can consciously tap into the lines of communication that have always been there with others.

Take a moment to recall all the groups you have been a member of, such as:

- Family
- Ex-families
- Relationships
- Ex-relationships
- Friendships
- Ex-friendships
- School groups or classes
- Sports associations
- Clubs
- Committees
- Companies/offices/places of employment

Every one of the groups you have been a member of has an over-soul. Think about your body and its organs as an example. The cells of your liver have an over-soul called the liver. Each cell is a member and is energetically connected. Your liver is a member of your body. All your organs, tissues, and muscles are members and are energetically connected. Your body is a member of all the groups you've subscribed to. Every person of each group is a member, and each is energetically connected.

Are the members of the groups aware of the connection? Some are, and some aren't. It depends on their level of awareness.

Are the cells of your big toe aware they are members of the same body as your brain cells? Maybe and maybe not; however, they are members—whether they have awareness or not. Similarly, you are still a member of every group and relationship you have connected with—whether you have awareness or not.

If you like it that way, you don't need to change anything. If you no longer want your energy going to groups and relationships that you have outgrown, you need to remove your energy and connection. If you don't, you will continue to be connected, and a percentage of your energy budget will continue to go to these groups.

Think of each group over-soul as a mandarin. You need to remove your segment, bring it back into yourself, and allow the space in the group over-soul mandarin to close over and readjust.

Exercise

You may need to allow extra time to do this exercise—especially if you are removing your energy from a relationship or group that has held a lot of emotional charge for you. Don't rush it. Take all the time you need. Be thorough and gentle with yourself. Every time you reclaim your energy from a group or relationship that is no longer appropriate for you, you are restoring your own power to yourself. All the energy you are calling back into yourself will then be available for use on your current and future projects and plans, rather than whittling away on projects you have no affinity with anymore.

Everyone has a number of group over-souls to re-claim their energy and power from. I recommend you reclaim yourself from one at a time. Pace yourself accordingly.

- Sit in your quiet space.
- Clear all negative energies from you and surround yourself with white light.
- Relax and close your eyes.
- Choose a particular group over-soul to work with and picture it as a mandarin with segments.
- Give thanks to the group over-soul and all its members for all it has given and taught you. You don't need to have a conscious recognition of what these gifts were, but if you would like to know, simply sit in your quiet space and ask. Allow the answers to come to you in whatever form they can (as a picture, idea, thought, words, feelings, etc.). You may actually find you feel more grateful if you indulge in this step and acknowledge the gifts—especially if the connection is one which hasn't been filled with totally loving memories.
- Remove your segment of mandarin and place it in your feeling centre or solar plexus.
- Allow the energy you have reclaimed to absorb and merge into place.
- Ask that your blueprint be re-patterned to accommodate the new energy.
- Close the gap in the group over-soul mandarin so there are no leakages of energy from there, and also ask that its blueprint be re-patterned to accommodate the change in state.
- Make certain you are grounded; extend your grounding cords back into the core of the earth if you feel at all lightheaded.
- When you're ready, open your eyes.

This is an exercise that everyone loves to do. It is a wonderful and gentle way to reclaim your power. You won't need any encouragement to work your way through your list, because you will feel better and better every time you reclaim yourself.

Some people also gain an awareness of what the exchange was when they do this process. Everything is a two-way street. The foot moves the brain to different locations, and the brain makes sure the foot doesn't stand on glass. You will have received valuable gifts and knowledge from each group you've been involved in, and they, too, will have benefited in some way from your contribution.

Make a commitment to yourself to reclaim your energy from a group on a regular basis. Set yourself a schedule and stick to it so you can reap the rewards.

12. Why Your Energy Is So Important

Your beliefs, thoughts, words, and actions determine your results. We've already discussed how everything that is happening in your life is a result of your beliefs, thoughts, words, and actions of the past. You know the process—but how and where does this happen in your body?

Modern physics tell us it happens everywhere. In the past, it was thought that your mind was in your brain; but the more we learn, the more we discover that your mind permeates every living cell in your body.

Your *mental body* is the energy pattern or template that surrounds and penetrates your whole being. This is where you hold the structure of your beliefs—much like a blueprint. As you change your beliefs, you change your blueprint and the structure of your mind—much like upgrading software in a computer.

Your blueprint or software program determines how you respond with your feelings and emotions.

Your feelings and emotions also have their own blueprints or software and are commonly referred to as your *feeling pattern* or *emotional body*. Feeling pattern and emotional body are like cantalope and rock melon. They are the same thing, but we can use different words to describe them.

Your emotional body reflects into your *etheric body,* which is the blueprint for your physical body. This means that your emotions directly influence your physical body—surprise, surprise.

Whatever you program into your etheric blueprint determines how your physical body functions. The more balanced your etheric blueprint, the stronger and healthier your physical body. If there are imbalances in your etheric, then you will have corresponding imbalances in your physical body directly in accordance with where the imbalances are. For example, if there's excess energy in the hormone control centres, you will have hormone excesses—and vice versa for deficiencies.

Your physical body is directly affected by your emotions and beliefs. Therefore, upgrading your software programs for your beliefs and emotions will concurrently improve your physical health and function.

You're the best person to reprogram or upgrade your thoughts and beliefs, because you're the person in charge of them.

Your energy bodies house your energy centres, called chakras. (*Chakra* is a Sanskrit word meaning "spinning wheel.") Chakras are "spinning wheels" of energy within your Master Diamond Blueprints and energy bodies. The chakras communicate between your energy bodies (including mental, emotional, and etheric) and your physical body. They also communicate with your physical body via your nervous system, which then communicates with your endocrine or hormone system and all of the muscles, tissues, organs, and every cell in your body.

This means your chakras or energy centres affect the performance of every cell in your body.

This means that everything you think, say, and do affects every cell in your body.

Hence you can see the importance of every level. All your energy bodies and physical body are inter-related, and your beliefs are at the top of your tree.

Your beliefs determine how you feel and respond emotionally. These programs are communicated via your chakras and the lines of energy that emanate from them to determine the quality and characteristics of your physical, emotional, and mental health.

You also have other energy bodies or blueprints (astral body, etheric template, celestial body, and ketheric body) that are the records of your experiences, and they determine aspects of your personality, talents, and challenges that you have chosen before birth. This is a reflection of the Law of Cause and Effect and is often referred to as *karma*.

Since the chakras are intermediaries between the different energy bodies, it can help you to understand how you function if you know what each one is related to.

You actually have many chakras, and some schools categorize them into major and minor. Older systems allocate seven chakras in the major category, and modern systems, nine or more. This doesn't mean that some systems are right or wrong; it just depends on the era. In the past, everyone was learning and progressing at much the same rate, whereas now we have huge variety. We now have people who are very psychically aware, developed, and "awake"; others who are very much unaware and "asleep"; and a wide range in between. Hence, we now have some people operating on their nine major and twenty-six minor chakra systems—and others still on their seven major and twenty-two minor chakra systems. There are many more chakras as well; however, these are the most relevant at this time.

Inner healing, meditation, and spiritual practices can develop and raise the vibration of your chakras like doing a physical workout develops your muscles and fitness. You may even have more strength or energy in some chakras compared to others.

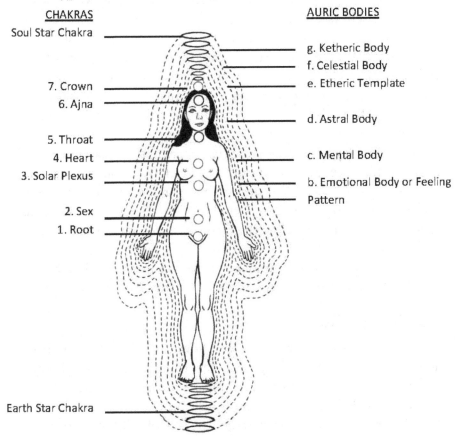

THE MAIN CHAKRAS AND AURIC BODIES

What's up Your Chakra?

Understanding what your chakras are associated with can give you profound insight and guidance as to where you can make changes in order to get your best results. When you know the purpose and functions of the chakras, you can work backward to pinpoint where your blockages are. Armed with this knowledge, you can then do something about it by changing the limiting beliefs and behaviors.

For example, if you know your base or root chakra controls structure and your skeleton and you have continual spinal problems, you will know you need to do clearing, repairing, energizing, or activating work on your base chakra in order to make lasting change. It is from the base or root chakra that the energy emanates to maintain your spine. Blockages in the root chakra limit and alter the flow of energy to the spine. You may also need to continue working on the spine itself as well as the organs and muscles associated with each vertebral level; however, a substantial starting point is with the chakra itself. It's the power station for everything associated with it. It doesn't matter how good the globe is; if the switch isn't turned on, the light won't shine. It doesn't matter how massaged the muscles are; if the root chakra isn't turned on, the right balances of contraction and relaxation won't happen.

Likewise, if you have constant sugar cravings, you can follow the chain back and see that you need to do work with your solar plexus chakra, because it is associated with sugar metabolism and your self-esteem or how sweet you view life to be. If you have problems speaking up, you can follow the chain back to your throat chakra, and so on.

There is a reasonable amount of overlap in the chakra system which allows for a backup when things go wrong.

Earth Star Chakra

This chakra has always been present; however, it hasn't always been activated or fully functioning. The new generations of mystics and warrior children that are now birthing are being born with this (and the soul star chakra above the head) fully functioning. The rest of us have had to learn and grow through the school of life to activate it.

Hence, there are many people with it fully functioning, others with it totally dormant, and variations in between.

It is located about six inches (fifteen centimeters) beneath your feet, in the ground.

Function: Its major function is to coordinate your grounding cord to anchor your master diamond blueprints into the core of the earth. It is associated with:

- Grounding your personal truth (compared with grounding what you have "learnt" from others—school, family, religion, courses, etc.).

You need to be functioning from your own truth for this chakra to fully activate and allow you to be fully grounded.

Foods that Can Help

Meat, protein, root vegetables, and red fruits and vegetables (tomatoes, cherries, red berries, red apples, peppers).

Chakra 1: Base/Root/Coccyx Chakra

Function: The major function of this chakra is to help you meet your basic needs for survival. This chakra activates and regenerates through physical movement. It is associated with:

- Security
- Safety
- Work
- Order
- Routine
- Nutrition
- Fairness
- Honesty
- Flexibility
- Responsibility
- Physical and mental health

Situations that cause us to "pull up our roots" create a deficiency in this chakra. In our modern world, these are often regular events—for example, moving house, traveling, changing jobs, and anything that triggers fear, such as changes in relationship, family, finances, career, or your body. Some people are so busy in their minds and active imaginations that they feel ungrounded most of the time. If you live in your head, you create imbalance in this chakra, which leads to "survival crises" such as illness, financial hardship, or housing challenge—anything that demands immediate attention.

Over-energized first chakras can create greed, hoarding of possessions or money, gaining excess weight—all in an effort to try and ground.

Associated Hormone Gland: Adrenals or Suprarenal Glands (make steroid hormones from cholesterol to deal with stress, including blood pressure and kidney function).

Physical: Grounding; adrenal and sex organs; skeleton, spine, and bones; physical health; blood; muscles; and general vitality.

Disease: Allergies, asthma, leukemia, sexual difficulties, low vitality, blood disorders, spinal problems, psychological problems (e.g., depression, suicidal moods), procrastination, impracticality, gullibility, unawareness.

People who have great brains but can't get the job done often have congested root chakras!

Daily Things You Can Do to Help this Chakra:

There are many simple things you can do every day to help this chakra and its associated issues.

- Clean, heal, energize, and activate it.
- Get organized and stay organized.
- Write down your intentions. (If you restrict yourself to writing goals, you can limit yourself to what you think you can have. Make sure you allow enough room for spirit to enter.)
- When you have inspired thoughts, take action on them. Follow through.

- Exercise. (When you move your body, you move your life. Do any exercise that is fun for you.)
- Eat protein.
- Eat root vegetables.
- Eat red foods (tomatoes, cherries, red berries, red apples, peppers).
- Organize your drawers (find new homes for the things you don't use).
- Clean your home.
- Clean your workplace.
- Get your spine adjusted and realigned.
- Walk with bare feet.
- Take your shoes off before you enter your home.
- Do grounding exercises.
- Cook your own meals.
- Listen to your body and honor its signals. (If you need to rest, exercise, meditation, to slow down, to speed up, or to drink more water, then do so.)
- Keep your integrity. Stay true to your own principles.
- Stand up for yourself.
- Garden (pull weeds and sow seeds).
- Keep your agreements and commitments.
- Have regular massages or reflexology.
- Make peace with everyone you're at odds with. Sometimes this means clearing the air first to allow true peace to enter. Start with yourself, your family, and people in your immediate environment.

Foods that Can Help

As for earth star chakra—meat, protein, root vegetables, red fruits and vegetables (tomatoes, cherries, red berries, red apples, peppers).

Daily Questions:

- Have I focused on abundance today?
- How can I improve my finances?

- What rewards have I given myself today?
- Have I exercised, relaxed, worked, and nourished myself today?
- Does my environment reflect me?

When your chakras become dirty, congested, or damaged, they cannot function at their peak, and problems will occur with the jobs they do and are responsible for. For example, if you don't have goals and are not actively engaged in their creation and learning from them, the energy will not flow properly through your root chakra. It will become dirty and congested, which will then perpetuate your lack of goals and direction and create difficulties with such things as your skeleton, including spine and joint problems; blood; psychology; and immune system.

If you don't create structure in your life, you will have problems with your physical structure.

Similarly, if you are annoyed with yourself for what you are doing or not doing, then you can be allergic to yourself and create sensitivities, especially to foods. *If you aren't nourishing yourself, you won't let food nourish you, either,* creating mal-absorption and assimilation problems.

Michael's Story

Michael was a dedicated healer and course facilitator. He was known for being highly focused and usually got a lot done. He committed to teaching others how to heal themselves with energy healing techniques that were compiled by Tom. He was so motivated to help others that he let go of his own goals and needs in order to perpetuate Tom's work. He didn't understand why he was developing food sensitivities to dairy and wheat. After all, he was following a spiritual path and working on himself as well as helping others to heal themselves!

He was already eating well, so he started taking herbs, vitamins, and pre- and post-biotics to help keep his body balanced. Michael also went to practitioners and gained a lot of assistance and relief. The symptoms were being kept under reasonable control but weren't totally resolving. The cause of the situation was still there!

It took some time to realize it was his base chakra and life direction that were out of balance, and this was causing all the trouble. Michael was diligently and generously promoting Tom's goals rather than his own! He was nourishing someone else at the expense of himself. Michael's food wasn't nourishing him, because he wasn't nourishing his own life. Equally interesting, Tom wasn't healthy, either. In fact, he was quite sick. He wasn't nourishing himself, because he was getting so much help from Michael and others he didn't realize the need to do it himself.

When Michael put his focus into his own goals and learnt fast and effective ways to clean and balance his chakras, he began to absorb his food efficiently again.

Jessica's Story

Jessica was a regular teenager.

It was coming to the time when she needed to make some clear decisions about what subjects to take to set up for her future, and she was having a hard time deciding. There were plenty of wise people in her life to advise her, but still she was confused. Whenever there is confusion, there is congestion in the base chakra.

I asked Jess about her room, and she said it was a mess. I explained that her environment was a reflection of her. When her base chakra was congested, her head and her environment would also get congested. When her base chakra was clean and tidy, her head and room could follow.

The relationship works in both directions. By cleaning her room and cleaning and energizing her base chakra, she cleared her mind. Once her mind was clear, she found it easier to choose.

Now she knows the signs. As soon as she feels confused, unmotivated, starts procrastinating, or feels depressed, she knows it's time to clean her base chakra and her immediate environment.

This is such a simple and powerful way to initiate change. Shifting the clutter shifts the energy.

When your base chakra is clean and activated, you will have a clear sense of life direction and a positivity that will help you set and attain your goals.

Chakra 2: Sacral/Sex Chakra

Function: The major functions of this chakra are to help you "create"; emotional and sensual vitality; sexuality, intimacy, and relationships; and abundance. This chakra activates and regenerates through connection to water.

The major functions of the second chakra are to help you create and allow emotional and sensual movement in your life, to open to pleasure, and learn how to go with the flow. It is involved with emotional and sensual vitality, sexuality, intimacy, desire, and relationships. All things "watery" are associated with this chakra (such as circulation, urination, menstruation, orgasm, and tears). Water flows, moves, and changes. When your second chakra is healthy, it allows you to do so too. Hence it is associated with:

- Relationships
- Intimacy
- Abundance
- Comfort
- Pleasure
- Romance
- Desire
- Beauty
- Passion
- Sensuality
- Affection
- Style
- Sexuality
- Indulgence
- Sweetness

Hormone Gland: Reproductive glands (ovaries or testes).

Physical: Sex organs, bladder, legs, magnetism, charisma, libido, hips, sacrum, lower back, genitals, uterus, bladder, and kidneys.

Disease: Sex-related problems, including impotence and frigidity, bladder disorders, aging, Alzheimer's disease, brain functions, and memory disorders.

Daily Things You Can Do to Help this Chakra

There are many simple things you can do every day to help this chakra and its associated issues.

- Clean, heal, energize, and activate this chakra.
- Do anything associated with water—bathe, swim, shower, scuba, surf.
- Affirm abundance in your life.
- Watch a romantic movie.
- Listen to sensuous music.
- Create (paint, draw, do crafts, cook, sew, do woodwork, build).
- Take a long bath with essential oils by candlelight.
- Make love.
- Have an aromatherapy massage.
- Eat orange foods (oranges, apricots, pumpkin, carrots, mangoes, kumara, cantaloupe, papaya, peaches).
- Arrange flowers in a vase .
- Burn essential oils.
- Watch a sunrise and/or sunset.
- Exfoliate and moisturize your skin (do it yourself or go to a spa).
- Walk in nature.
- Do a meditation affirming your interconnection to all things.

Foods that Can Help

Liquids, orange foods (oranges, carrots, pumpkin, apricots, cantalope, mangoes, peaches, papaya, kumara).

Daily Questions

- Did I embrace change today?
- What did I create today?
- Did I respect my male and female today (soft and assertive)?
- Did I give and receive today?

When you forget you are connected to everyone and everything, you create a feeling of separateness, and this can create blockages and damage to your second or reproductive chakra.

As soon as you think you are separate, you go into competition, and this creates struggle. You will feel like you are either better than others or not as good as others, and it will seem like there is always something to win. This naturally creates difficulties in your relationships.

When you aren't getting your needs met, you will feel stressed and start blaming others.

Congestion here also creates poverty consciousness, hormone imbalance, libido problems, premenstrual syndrome, or "poor me" syndrome.

When your second chakra is unbalanced, you can tend to avoid, control, or ignore your feelings. You may even disconnect from sensuality altogether. By severing yourself from your sensuality and your feelings, you end up living life "in your head." If the imbalance gets worse, your "shadows" can run amok and put an end to all spontaneity, pleasure, and joy.

Julie's Story

Julie grew up in a male-dominated home with brothers who made it clear to her they considered males superior. This was a double-edged sword for Julie. It was good in the context it made her strive but it was a challenge in that her whole life became a competition. When she was winning, she felt good enough to fit in, but if she came second or less, she felt inadequate. Everything she did was an unconscious attempt to show she wasn't inferior.

Julie became a high achiever from an early age. She didn't like to lose. It wasn't the need to feel better than others that drove her, but the acute desire to feel good about herself and to receive approval.

Competition creates stress and actually stops you from getting your needs met. Not getting your needs met creates poor me syndrome or PMS. Julie had severe PMS and difficulties with relationships.

Julie learnt to focus on the things that balanced her sex chakra. She consciously chose to create a sense of belonging and did creative things just for the fun of it and for her own self-improvement rather than to win, be better than anyone else, or gain approval. In time, her hormone and relationship issues began to ease. When she allowed herself to have fun and feel like she belonged, she discovered better ways of relating—not just with others, but also more gently with herself.

Julie actually became grateful for her blockages rather than blaming her childhood situation because she learnt so much and grew as a whole person because of it.

Chakra 3: Solar Plexus Chakra

Function: This chakra governs self-direction, personal will, intention, self-responsibility, self-control, self-esteem (and hence the power of transformation), digestion, and metabolism. This chakra activates and regenerates through connection to crystals. It is associated with:

- Self-esteem
- Personal power
- Decision-making
- Focus
- Commitment
- Boundaries
- Authority
- Cooperation
- Integrity
- Choice
- Discipline
- Courage
- Faith
- Intention
- Willingness

A deficient solar plexus chakra can result in excess weight around your middle and appetite change; codependency (making decisions based on pleasing others rather than pleasing yourself); fear of rejection, disapproval, or abandonment; addiction; and suppressed anger.

An over-energized solar plexus chakra can cause too much sovereignty, narrow-mindedness, intimidation, insensitivity, aggression, an inability to stop or slow down, and workaholism.

Hormone Gland: Pancreas.

Physical: Pancreas, liver, diaphragm, small and large intestines, appendix, stomach, self-esteem, and personal identity.

Disease: Diabetes, ulcers, irritable bowel syndrome, hepatitis, gall bladder disease, heart problems, high cholesterol, tension, stress, fear, anger, worry, hate, poor self-image, lack of persistence, unassertiveness, and victim consciousness.

Daily Things You Can Do to Help this Chakra

There are many simple things you can do every day to help this chakra and its associated issues.

- Clean, heal, energize, and activate it.
- Write a mission statement for yourself. Get clear about your intentions.
- Curb sugar and carbohydrate habits.
- Sleep on things before you commit to them.
- If you don't want to do something, say so.
- If you mean "no," don't say "yes."
- Get a planner diary and use it.
- Each night, write your intentions for the next day.
- Eat yellow foods (bananas, lemons, squash, corn).
- Give genuine compliments (to yourself as well as others).
- Take a class on time management and leadership. (Work smarter, not harder.)
- Do anger release processes.
- Only share your plans with people who support you. (Avoid naysayers.)
- Re-vamp your wardrobe.
- Read biographies of successful people.
- Listen to motivational tapes or CDs and take action on what they inspire in you.

- Get a mentor or life coach who understands the higher truth of intention rather than just goal-setting.

Foods that Can Help

Complex carbohydrates, yellow foods (lemons, bananas, squash, corn).

Daily Questions

- Were you true to yourself today?
- How did you express your anger today?
- Did you act with confidence today?

How you feel about your likes and dislikes, successes, and failures is expressed through your solar plexus chakra. Feelings of failure and low self-esteem create blockages here, and this creates a need to find sweetness.

When you feel angry or give yourself a hard time, you create blockages here. This causes problems with all the organs and functions associated with it, including inconsistence, lack of commitment, poor self-image, and blood sugar swings, including diabetes.

Diabetes is now a major and growing problem in the western world. These people are suffering consequences of mood swings, loss of vision, infections, ulcers, kidney problems, and amputations—which may have begun from imbalance in their third chakra.

David's Story

David had a sweet tooth. Whenever he felt tired or his were feelings low, he would eat sweet things in an effort to feel better. And it worked—temporarily! In the short term, he would feel the sugar-induced high, but unfortunately, this was inevitably followed by the impending low blood sugar slump. His mood had no option but to slump as well.

The slumps would then trigger more sugar cravings, which caused him to eat even more in an effort to ward off the slump. And so the downward spiral continued.

The sugar fed the organisms in David's bowel and led to an overgrowth of bacteria, yeasts, and moulds. This initiated Candida and parasite infestations, which also perpetuated his sugar cravings. (Candida lives on sugar, so if you starve it of sugar, it will scream for more. You have to starve it; kill off the excess with things like garlic, onion, Pau D'Arco, Artemesia, or Black Walnut; and replenish the friendly bacteria such as Lactobacillus, acidophilus, and Bifidobacterium lactis to keep it in check.) Parasitic overgrowth interferes with the efficient absorption of essential nutrients (this creates vitamin and mineral deficiencies which lead to constant colds, loss of sex drive, fluid retention, blood pressure changes, hormonal imbalance, etc.) and sets off food sensitivities.

Before long, David had a digestive disaster, a mood swing roller coaster, and a distinct lack of concentration on his hands. Every time he went off the rails with sugar, his personal boundaries got vague. Quite possibly, the reverse was also true—when his personal boundaries got vague, he went off the rails with sugar.

David began looking to other people for advice and to make decisions for him. He didn't feel confident making decisions and gave his power to others to make them for him. Buyer's remorse was also prevalent. When he finally made a decision, he would then second-guess his choice and get even more confused, wondering if he'd taken the best option.

David learnt to clean and energize his solar plexus chakra daily. It was only a short time before his self-esteem, personal boundaries and commitment began to improve. This kept his blood sugar balanced and supported his decision-making and self confidence.

Keeping your own counsel is really important. It is part of accepting and being responsible for yourself and your life. This doesn't mean you should ignore the advice of wise mentors; it simply means make your own decisions and be accountable to yourself.

Chakra 4: Heart Chakra

Function: Governs all aspects of love (giving, receiving, losing, regaining), feelings of compassion, forgiveness, understanding, generosity, empathy, and caring. This chakra activates and regenerates through the breath. It is associated with:

- Empathy
- Generosity
- Compassion
- Forgiveness
- Acceptance
- Unconditional love
- Tolerance
- Affection
- Kindness
- Patience
- Laughter

When your heart chakra is balanced, you accept yourself and others without judging, find it easy to overlook weaknesses, are kind and quick to forgive, tolerant, optimistic, resourceful, and humorous.

If your heart centre is shut down, you'll have a tendency to avoid intimacy. Unfortunately, without this sense of connection, you can become critical, suspicious, and defensive. By closing your heart, you push people away, which naturally causes them to reject you and seemingly validate your situation. Again you pull back, and again you're pushed away in a self-fulfilling prophecy. Your heart becomes more closed, and you become more isolated.

If your heart chakra is too wide open, you can become too empathic—too easily picking up on the anger or depression of others. This causes you to live at the mercy of the moods and feelings of the people around you—which is psychically and physically draining!

Hormone Gland: Thymus.

Physical: Heart, thymus, circulatory system, lungs.

Disease: Heart disease, circulation, and lung problems, including asthma. Anxiety, agitation, lack of reception to healing, unhappiness, feeling unloved, inability to find inner peace.

Daily Things You Can Do to Help this Chakra

There are many simple things you can do every day to help this chakra and its associated issues.

- Clean, heal, energize, and activate it.
- Watch a love story.
- Give a hug.
- Receive a hug.
- Read poetry.
- Write poetry.
- Write thank-you notes.
- Apologize to people you've hurt.
- Forgive the people you hold grudges against—start with your parents and yourself.
- Offer to help.
- Ask for help.
- Allow yourself to be helped.
- Send flowers.
- Spend time in nature.
- Do a healing workshop.
- Be grateful.
- Donate the clothes you don't wear to welfare.
- Donate the time you don't use to someone who needs you.

Foods that Can Help

Vegetables, green foods (broccoli, cabbage, lettuce family, beans, peas, limes, spouts, grasses, cucumber, courgettes, chokoes, asparagus).

Daily Questions

- Were you compassionate today?

- Were you compassionate with yourself today?
- Did you give love today?
- Did you receive love today?

If you have problems acquiring, releasing, giving, or receiving love, it is a sign that you have an imbalance in your heart chakra.

How you feel about others is often a reflection of how you feel about yourself. As long as you don't love yourself, you won't find it in others—even though it's already there. It's there, but you won't see it. You'll feel unhappy, unloved, and anxious. Inner peace will be elusive, and you won't be receptive to healing. When you begin to love yourself and see love in yourself, you will see and feel it from others. You will see what was always there.

You can be honest without being harsh—and this is equally important to remember when dealing with yourself. It is one thing to see where you need to change and another to dislike yourself for it. Allow yourself the love and forgiveness you deserve. If you don't think you deserve it, allow yourself to feel worthy, so that in turn, you will come to know you deserve love.

Let go of everything that is holding you back. Keep your own counsel, and don't give your power away to other peoples' negative opinions. Especially, don't be influenced in how to feel about yourself—unless it is positive.

When you truly know what you want and are devoted to yourself, you won't allow your heart to sink, because you'll have your own yardstick to measure yourself by. This is far more appropriate than someone else's judgments that have nothing to do with who you really are.

Patrick's Story

Patrick was a divorcee with four young children. Any spare time that wasn't devoted to work was consumed by them. He was a somewhat successful executive. He was good at his job, although he didn't always clinch the big deals and was considered hard to get along with.

He met someone new, but kept her at a distance, as he did his workmates and family members other than his children. His relationship, work, and friendships were all in holding patterns. They kept him safe but were going nowhere.

I reminded him that *what anyone else thought of him was none of his business* and that it was what he thought of himself that was important.

I taught him how to clean his congested heart chakra and to forgive himself for leaving his wife and family. The guilt had kept him shackled for four years. Once he forgave himself and healed his heart chakra, he could allow others close again. Business improved, relationships improved, and he started to laugh again.

~~~

The biggest stumbling block for heart chakra healing is usually un-forgiveness. When you hold anger and un-forgiveness in your, heart it prevents you from giving and receiving love. Forgiveness has to come from your whole heart—not just the logical concept from your head. You'll know you've truly forgiven someone when you're happy to be in the same room with them and there is no longer a charge in it.

When your heart chakra is clean and activated, you will not only forgive your alleged perpetrators and give and receive love easily, you will also develop clairsentience (i.e., your sense of knowing will increase and gut feelings will get clearer and stronger). You may not know how you know or even why you know, but you will know.

Life is a journey. Take one step at a time, and keep stepping.

Chakra 5: Throat Chakra

Function: The major function of this chakra is to govern communication and your personal expression. This chakra is activated and regenerated by expressing your truth. It is associated with:

- Speaking
- Singing
- Listening
- Writing

- Drawing
- Rapport
- Revealing
- Expressing your opinions and personal truths

A deficiency in your throat chakra creates neck stiffness, shoulder tension, teeth grinding, jaw problems, throat disorders, underactive thyroid, and a fear of speaking.

An over-energized throat chakra causes excessive talking, inability to listen, hearing difficulties, stuttering, and overactive thyroid problems.

Hormone Gland: Thyroid.

Physical: Throat, thyroid, and parathyroid glands. Hearing, speaking, lymphatics, and organizational abilities.

Disease: Throat problems (e.g., sore throat, loss of voice), goiter, asthma. Not speaking up for yourself; not speaking your truth; lack of attention to detail; difficulty managing, studying, categorizing, and planning.

Daily Things You Can Do to Help this Chakra

There are many simple things you can do every day to help this chakra and its associated issues.

- Clean, heal, energize, and activate it.
- Speak positively.
- Greet people in a positive manner.
- Breathe before you speak.
- Sing in the car, shower, bath, etc.
- Hum. (Humming actually strengthens the lines of energy in your etheric blueprint).
- If you think or say anything negative, immediately "cancel" it and send it to the universal white light for transformation.
- Write. (Keep a journal; write your biography; write your opinion to magazines, newspapers, and chat rooms.)
- Draw. (Doodle, sketch, color in, etc.)
- Paint. (Have fun—use brushes or finger paint.)

- Laugh.
- Take a public speaking course.
- Participate in conversations.
- Have an opinion.
- Meditate in silence for ten to twenty minutes each day.

Foods that Can Help

Fruits, blue foods (blueberries, plums).

Daily Questions

- Did I sing, chant, hum, or whistle today?
- Did I express my feelings today?
- Did I hold my neck in good posture today?

Kathy's Story

Kathy was multi-talented. She was a gifted healer, had good organization and computer skills, and had a wide network of friends. Even though she was good at what she did and knew a variety of people, she always found promoting herself, social occasions, and particularly intimate relationships difficult. She confessed she never knew what to say, or she would think of what was appropriate afterwards—when the timing was no longer suitable.

She hadn't always been this way but had been misinterpreted and considered offensive on occasion, and she became progressively more reluctant to speak up. She began to have bouts of sore throat, tonsillitis, and neck pain and was getting checked for thyroid dysfunction.

Kathy learnt to clean and energize her throat chakra, and expression became easier. Initially, she found that writing was effortless, so she gained her confidence in expressing herself here and made progressive steps to verbalize her opinions. The more she got to know her own truth, the easier it was to communicate with others.

~~~

The more relaxed you are, the easier it is to communicate your truth and wisdom. If you worry about what other people think of you, then you'll have trouble speaking up and will give yourself throat and neck problems. If you notice your throat becoming tight, dry, or sore, use this as an indicator that you actually have something to say which you are holding back.

Find a way to express what you really want to say. *When you are truly speaking from your heart, you will not be offensive, and people will hear what you are expressing.*

The more you speak your personal truth in an appropriate manner, the easier your throat chakra spins, which helps you to continue speaking up. It's a self-perpetuating spiral.

You may find that if you feel confused, have trouble making decisions, or behave irrationally, it is your throat chakra that needs cleaning.

It is foolish to assume that other people know what you want if you haven't expressed it. Practice toning in the car; sing the vowels *(a, e, i, o, u)* or "ohm" repeatedly. Ignore the sound and focus on the feeling in your body. Keep repositioning yourself until you can't feel any restrictions. You might surprise yourself with how good you actually sound.

When your throat chakra is clean and activated, you'll speak and communicate clearly and easily, and you will pay more attention to details. This also develops your clairaudient skills—your ability to hear your inner voice and higher guidance.

Chakra 6: Third Eye/Ajna Chakra

Function: Governs your ability to think, reason, understand, discern, analyze, dream, imagine, and visualize. This chakra is activated and regenerated by connecting to and living in alignment with your higher purpose. It is associated with:

* Perception
* Discernment
* Imagination
* Visualization (and the ability to create positive pictures of your future)

- Dreams
- Memory
- Clairvoyance
- Insight
- Open-mindedness
- Reasoning
- Thinking
- Opinion

When your third eye chakra is deficient, it causes poor memory, eye and vision problems, difficulty recognizing patterns, and difficulty visualizing clearly.

When the third eye is over-energized, it causes headaches, nightmares, and difficulty concentrating.

Hormone Gland: Pineal. (People who live by their own personal philosophy have their pineal gland associated with their third eye chakra. People who follow external philosophies such as rigid religious beliefs have their pituitary gland associated here.)

Physical: Brain and pineal gland, eyes, ears, nervous system, the ability to understand abstract concepts and principles.

Disease: Cancer, allergies, asthma, and hormonal imbalances, chaotic emotions, allowing other people to control you.

Daily Things You Can Do to Help this Chakra

There are many simple things you can do every day to help this chakra and its associated issues.

- Clean, heal, energize, and activate it.
- Meditate.
- Put a positive greeting on your mobile phone.
- Write a positive affirmation on your screen saver and change it regularly.
- Develop your memory; play memory games.
- Look for details you haven't noticed before.
- Keep a journal of your positive experiences.
- Smile every time you see your reflection.

- Visualize yourself succeeding.
- Visualize yourself having a great day before you get out of bed.
- Look for good.
- Feng Shui your home and work place.

Foods that Can Help

Eggplant (aubergine), passion fruit.

Daily Questions

- Did you act on your intuition today?
- Did you notice what was around you today (colors, shapes, details)?

Your third eye chakra is the window to your soul. It is through this place that you have access to your inner visions and your life purpose. Your soul will show you through this place the direction it wants you to go. You are not separate from your soul; it is a part of you, and you are a part of it.

Alison's Story

Alison was committed to living her life purpose—the only problem was, she wasn't sure what her life purpose was! She sought wise council from friends, attended multiple self-development courses, and had in-depth discussions with respected intuits. Everyone had a higher vision for her than what she believed she was living. Her librarian role didn't seem to match the picture of educator and leader that people said was her path.

Alison continued to meditate on her purpose and assess her direction, but she felt just as confused as ever. She would have glimpses of changes she needed to make, but fear stopped her from following through. She would have work to complete and deadlines to meet, but would irrationally fritter away her time on something else. Her actions were destructive, but she continued to do them anyway.

The less she trusted herself, the more congested her sixth chakra became—which simply created more confusion and clouded reasoning.

Alison felt resentful and felt an injustice had been done. She was prepared to follow a dream but was angry that the universe appeared not to support her.

As time passed, Alison's frustration grew, and she was even more aghast to be diagnosed with breast cancer.

The primary blockage for many people with cancer is in their third eye or ajna centre. I had seen many patients benefit greatly from clearing and rebalancing here. Not only do the blockages need to be removed, but also the faulty thinking behind them.

Cleaning, healing, and re-energizing Alison's third eye helped stabilize her health an opened her up to knowing her own purpose rather than looking to others for guidance. The clearer she got on what she wanted to do, the easier it was to visualize herself already doing it, and her health and fulfillment spirals both turned for the better.

~~~

The truth of why the situation occurred and the benefits of the experience needed to be seen, rather than sinking into the resentment and bitterness that resulted from it. This was confronting, as it required complete honesty; however, the benefits far outweighed the stagnation from delusion.

If you believe something to suit your own agenda when it isn't really the truth, it causes problems in your ajna centre. Vice versa, when you have congestion here, it will perpetuate delusional thoughts that keep you from seeing a more useful perspective.

When your third eye chakra is clean and activated, you will have clear thoughts and an awareness of your inner vision. This will also help the development of your clairvoyant qualities.

Chakra 7: Crown Chakra

Function: Connects you to your source. It is the chakra for your spiritual consciousness and higher thinking. This chakra activates and regenerates by connecting to your source energy and recognizing your own divinity.

Associated with: Spiritual awareness.

A deficiency in your crown chakra makes it hard for you to think for yourself and causes apathy, skepticism, and materialism.

An over-energized crown chakra creates spiritual or intellectual snobbery—feeling you are a member of a spiritual or intellectual elite.

Hormone Gland: Pituitary. (People who live by their own personal philosophy have their pituitary gland associated with their crown chakra. People who follow external philosophies such as rigid religious beliefs have their pineal gland associated here.)

Physical: Pituitary and endocrine glands, overall grasp of things you couldn't know logically, knowledge and ideas.

Disease: Brain, psychological problems, and hormonal imbalances. When deficient, lack of inspiration, confusion, depression, alienation from the Divine, hesitation to serve, and senility. When over-energized, depression, migraines, headaches, frustration, psychoses, and bipolar disorders.

Daily Things You Can Do to Help this Chakra

There are many simple things you can do every day to help this chakra and its associated issues.

- Clean, heal, energize, and activate it.
- Meditate first thing in the morning.
- Be grateful; find at least three things to appreciate before sleeping every night.
- Listen to Gregorian chanting.
- Bless your food.
- Bless yourself.
- Talk to God.
- Listen to God.
- Light a candle and dedicate it with positive intention.
- Visit sacred sites.
- Write to your higher guidance, asking for help on your path.

- Write from your higher guidance with your non-dominant hand.
- Take up spiritual practices that you align with.
- Have a day of rest every week.
- Sponsor or adopt a needy child.

Foods that Can Help

Walnuts, purple foods (plums, grapes, figs).

Daily Questions

- Did you identify yourself with you today (as compared to your job, material attributes, etc.)?
- Were you open to magic in your life today?
- Did you meditate today?

If you don't notice the higher guidance of your spirit, there is a blockage in your crown chakra. Your guides, guardian angels, or spiritual helpers can never leave you. If you aren't aware of their presence, it is simply because you aren't allowing it. Often this means your fears are simply getting in the way and preventing you from noticing.

Have you ever felt totally alone, even though there may have been a number of people around you? This may help you understand that even though you may have felt that way, it wasn't actually the case. Often if you are feeling alone, it is when you're allowing doubt to enter.

Doubt is an acronym for Driving Ourselves Unconscious By Thinking.

Dean's Story

Dean was a thinker. He was a good thinker—too good! He would analyze every situation, turning conversations and actions inside out and upside down, trying to understand and interpret what meant what. He would think so deeply that he denied his feelings and would regularly sink into self-doubt and loneliness.

He was driving himself unconscious by thinking and losing sight of the truth that he had a lot to be confident about and a network of friends and family to support him. The constant frustration of everyday life pushed him to learn how to keep his crown chakra clean and activated. He began to be more patient with himself again, and over time, he was able to listen to and maintain his spiritual awareness.

~~~

Many traditional philosophies and teachings about chakras list the pituitary as being associated with the sixth chakra and the pineal with the seventh rather than the other way around.

As we grow and develop from learning common philosophies as dictated by the civilization of the time (this often meant the church) into seeking and living our own personal philosophies, the "wiring" of our master diamond blueprint changes. When we live by our own truth rather than just accepting the opinion of mass consciousness, we link our pineal to our sixth chakra and pituitary to the seventh.

Soul Star Chakra

As with the earth star chakra beneath your feet, this chakra has always been present; however, it hasn't always been activated or fully functioning. The new generations of mystics and warrior children are now born with this fully activated, whereas the rest of us have had to learn and grow through spiritual alignment and committing to the greater good. Hence, there are many people with it fully functioning, others with it totally dormant, and variations in between.

Function: The major function of this chakra is to ground your soul into your master diamond blueprints. This chakra activates and regenerates by reconnecting to your soul. It is associated with:

*   Soul healing
*   The dark night of the soul

Foods that Can Help

As for Chakra 7—Walnuts, purple foods (plums, grapes, figs).

~~~

As we continue to strive, grow, and return to love, we'll activate even more chakras that are currently dormant.

13. Chakra Clearing

Your chakras directly influence the quality of your physical, emotional, and mental well-being. The better shape they are in, the better shape you will be in.

It is essential to clean your energy bodies and chakras as regularly as you do your physical body.

If you have poor hygiene with your physical body, you will become a breeding ground for infection, smell unpleasant, and people won't want to be around you. If you have poor energy hygiene, filling yourself with physical and emotional toxins and not detoxing, you will also be a breeding ground for parasites, yeasts, moulds, bacteria, and fungi. This can lead to poor assimilation of the food you eat and create all sorts of nutritional and hormonal disorders.

If you have poor energy hygiene, your chakras will become congested, not spin correctly, and lead to all manner of mental, emotional, and physical complaints.

If your chakras are toxic, everything that is fed by them—including nerve plexuses, hormone-producing glands, and organs—will deteriorate and malfunction.

Just as your physical body gets dirty from the everyday processes of living, so too do your energy bodies—and they must be cleaned accordingly.

In the following process, you will not only clean your chakras, but their webs as well. Inside each chakra is a web that functions a bit like a filter or grease trap. A lot of the dirty energies get caught in here, so it is essential to do a thorough job of cleaning these as well.

How to Clean Your Chakras Simply and Easily

This might appear a bit involved at first, so simply take it step by step until you become familiar with it. Once you get the idea, you'll realize it's actually quite easy. Learning to walk was a bit tricky at first, but you can probably do that easily now—and if you persist with your chakra clearing, it will be that way, too.

- Rest comfortably in a quiet place where you won't be disturbed.
- Relax and gently close your eyes.
- Send your grounding cords down into the earth and connect up to your higher guidance.
- Clear yourself as you have already learnt to do so you rinse off the easy "dirt" and prevent more from coming in while you clean the denser grime away. Simply wash all the negative energies up to the white light above your head.
- Protect yourself. Surround yourself with the universal white light of protection. Surround yourself with the bright white light of Source coming from above your head. Shine it so that it totally encompasses you, including underneath your feet.
- Mentally place yourself within a cone of white light so that all the dense energies you release will be returned to source for transformation, much like going up an exhaust fan.
- Thoroughly wash the color violet through all of your energy bodies and chakras. Violet is the frequency that removes emotional blockages. (If you feel comfortable working with archangels, angels, and ascended masters, call upon St. Germaine and Lady Portia to help you with this cleansing process. They are the keepers of the violet flame and can assist you should you ask to run this frequency through your blueprints.)
- You can assist this cleansing process by affirming something like:

  o "I call upon St. Germaine and Lady Portia and ask them to use the violet flame to remove all negative energies from my entire mind, body, and spirit through all time, space, and dimensions."

- ○ "I command that all negative thoughts, thought forms, and thought form entities be dissolved and disintegrated, extracted and expelled from my entire soul, mind, and body now."
- ○ "I command that all negative thoughts, thought forms, and thought form entities; etheric parasites; all negative beliefs; all limiting beliefs; all negative vibrations; all wedges, barbs, and blockages; all fear, judgment, and un-forgiveness; and all that has gone to cause this be dissolved and disintegrated, extracted, and expelled from my entire mind, body, and spirit through all time, space, and dimensions now."

Include in your affirmation whatever you specifically choose to be free of. Be as extensive or intensive as you like. It's your own level of focus that determines how successful you'll be at what you're asking for. As with everything, the stronger your focus and belief in what you're doing, the better your results will be. The underlying principles or laws of the universe are the same. It makes no difference what you apply them to.

I recommend you do a quick clean of all of your energy bodies first and then be more specific and thorough, cleaning all major chakras individually.

- You can use your hand (take your jewelry off) to help you focus on what you are doing and to direct violet light specifically into the chakra you are cleaning. (Refer to the chakra chart for the chakras' locations.) *To remove dirty energies, point your fingers toward the chakra you are clearing, rotate your hand anti-clockwise, and direct the violet color into the chakra as you do so.*
- When you have taken energy out of a space, it is important to replace it with clean and positive energy—or else you will leave a hole. *To replace the energy you have removed, point your fingers at the chakra you are energizing and rotate your hand clockwise, sending white light into the chakra to re-energize it.*

- Ask for each chakra to be sealed before you move on to cleaning the next one so that the positive energy you have filled it with doesn't leak away.
- Continue cleaning all of the chakras.
- An attitude of gratitude is always helpful. Give thanks for the assistance you have received from your spirit helpers.

It is essential to clean your chakras thoroughly and regularly—otherwise you won't get the maximum benefit out of everything else you do. For example, you can avoid the foods you are sensitive to; take acidophilus, bifidus, and caseii until the cows come home; and get regular spinal adjustments—but if your base chakra is congested, you will not heal the cause of your food sensitivity, and you'll keep creating the same spinal subluxations over and over.

You will be able to control the symptoms if you are diligent at your practices, but they will always linger or recur if you don't repair and take care of your energetic blueprint. It is essential to do your deep inner healing and allow forgiveness of all that has gone to cause your wounds for complete healing to occur.

Using this violet flame technique is one of the fastest ways to shift your mood when you are wallowing in your muck. Get into the habit of cleaning yourself as a routine practice so you don't sink so low to begin with, and you can also use it to lift yourself up faster and easier when you do.

It's hard to teach a drowning man to swim. The more adept you are at using your skills on a day-to-day basis, the easier it will be for you when you are feeling pressured and really need to do it more than ever. Don't wait until you're drowning in emotion to learn how to clean your chakras.

Be aware the more you think about something, the more you perpetuate it—so don't be overly focused on what you perceive to be wrong or blocked. If you keep thinking your chakras, arteries, creativity, or any other things are blocked, you will create more blocks.

The same principle applies if you want something to go away. If you want a problem, pain, memory, or anything else to go away, you get more of it, too. You get more of what you think about.

Acknowledge what the difficulty is and what has gone to create it, and release it to the light for transformation.

Your difficulties, issues, and challenges are there for a reason. Often you created them to protect yourself.

If an adult hit you when you were small, it's a reasonable decision to back away from adults. However, things obviously change with time. As you become an adult yourself, the decision from the past is outdated and actually in the way. Rather than being a useful protection, it can now inhibit and stop you from interacting effectively with your fellow man and getting the fulfillment from your life you want and deserve.

This same principle applies to most fears, resentments, angers, and resistances. Those feelings are there because they were useful to you in the past. You put them in place to keep you safe. They aren't, however, necessarily applicable anymore.

The great thing about childhood is that it's over! Now you're an adult, and it's your responsibility to update your own software! You need to sort through and appropriately discard that which is no longer appropriate for you. Release the past and let it go.

14. Heal Your Heart

Many problems and blockages to healing are because of lack of forgiveness.

When you don't forgive on all levels of your heart, mind, and soul, the seeds of resentment continue to grow. The problem with these seeds is that they don't stay seeds. They become weeds, giant trees, or even forests if you keep feeding them with your thoughts, memories, and judgments. If you really want to heal and stop your problems, stop talking and thinking about them! Focus on the solution, not the problem—or else the problem has no choice but to grow!

One of the major areas of your body that stores un-forgiveness (and hence blocks your healing) is your heart (and heart chakra). If your heart is clogged by anger, resentment, frustration, and un-forgiveness, then it is not free to be the impetus in what you do, so neither you nor projects can flourish. You will not get the results you desire in life until the vibration of your heart centre matches your positive intentions. It's all about energy! If the vibration isn't a match, it isn't a match. You can't trick the universe or bluff your way through. The energy either matches or it doesn't.

If you are putting a lot of effort into your tasks and don't feel you are getting the corresponding rewards, then look to your heart chakra and check that it is clear and your intentions are pure. When your projects are intended for the good of all rather than just to make you rich, famous, or any other self-gratifying purpose, they can thrive.

You have probably heard of things pulling at your heartstrings when there is over-emotion about something. Within your master diamond blueprint for the heart chakra, you actually have heartstrings (or fibers or heart filaments, as they are also known).

When your heartstrings have been overtaxed by excess emotion, they stretch; in the extreme, they can actually break! Needless to say, all your attempts to heal are then limited at best and even halted until these heart filaments are healed again.

Your heartstrings resonate to particular notes—hence, when you are aligned with your heart, your heart "sings." When you have broken heartstrings or strings that are at the wrong tension and not resonating to their true notes, you cannot express your heart song.

Sometimes heartstrings heal as best they can and reconnect to the wrong place like a scar. Even though they may resonate and produce a tune, so to speak, it is not your true heart sound anymore. It feels like your heart's not in it anymore.

In the following exercise, you will *heal you heart filaments and painful scars* from the wounds you have encountered—*without any confrontation*. There's no need for you to relive any painful memories in this exercise! If the original pain was bad enough to damage your heart filaments in the first place, why would you want to relive it? Reliving it feeds it and can make it grow rather than dispersing it.

It is actually common to feel a bit euphoric and certainly full of the energies of love and peace after doing this exercise. With this in mind, it is a good idea to set yourself a time frame—say, half an hour—for its completion so you stay grounded.

Too much euphoria can be just as unbalancing as too much frustration. I agree that it is decidedly more enjoyable; however, you will be a lot more productive in your physical world if you are grounded rather than "off with the fairies."

I encourage you to heal progressively and completely rather than go for short-term quick fixes. You can't build a skyscraper on wet cement, so heal as much as you feel is right at any given time, allow it to settle, and then repeat the exercises to heal to your next layer.

I feel very confident that you will want to work with this exercise on an ongoing basis, because it feels so good and the benefits can be astounding. Healing your heart so you can "put your heart into" whatever you're doing again is a wonderful gift.

Tail Wagging the Dog

Until you truly heal your whole heart, you will be compelled to rely on your logic and your head, because your intuition will remain elusive or distorted. Damaged heart filaments deny you access to your intuition and inner knowing, and they deny you full healing of your soul.

When your heart is whole, you can intuit what to do and where to go. You can then use your head and logic to back your intuition rather than the other way around. The dog can wag the tail again!

How to Repair Your Heart Filaments

This exercise also helps you connect to, heal, and open your heart center. Your energy is always moving. It is either expanding or contracting. When your heart is open, your energy can expand with ease. When your heart is closed, you will naturally tend to close or contract and block your growth.

Exercise

Prepare yourself and your environment appropriately so you are comfortable and won't be disturbed.

- Clear yourself and your environment of all negativity.
- Protect yourself and the room you're in with the universal white light of positivity.
- Connect to your higher guidance and ask for assistance.
- Put yourself in a cone of light so any debris released is removed from you and sent to the light for transformation.
- Give yourself permission to heal.
- Uncross your arms and legs so you have free energy flow through and around your body. The more open you are (within your cleared and protected space), the more completely you can heal yourself.

These are essential setup steps prior to doing any meditation, inner work, or healing exercise (including going to a practitioner).

- Keep your breathing slow and steady, and go at your own pace. With your next breath, breathe in through the front of your chest and into your heart. For the whole of this exercise, continue to breathe through the front of your chest and into your heart.
- With your next breath, breathe in through the front of your chest, and expand your heart energy out to the *front*. Do this for three slow, steady breaths.
- With your next breath, breathe in through the front of your chest, and expand your heart energy out to the *back*. Do this for three slow, steady breaths.
- With your next breath, breathe in through the front of your chest, and expand your heart energy out to the *right*. Do this for three slow, steady breaths.
- With your next breath, breathe in through the front of your chest, and expand your heart energy out to the *left*. Do this for three slow, steady breaths.
- With your next breath, breathe in through the front of your chest, and expand your heart energy out to the *bottom*. Do this for three slow, steady breaths.
- With your next breath, breathe in through the front of your chest, and expand your heart energy out to the *top*. Do this for three slow, steady breaths.
- With your next breath, breathe in through the front of your chest, and expand your heart energy *in all directions simultaneously*. Expand your heart chakra energy to about two meters past your body, and keep it stable. Do this for three slow, steady breaths.
- Continue to breathe through the front of your chest, and ask for the cleansing and clearing, repairing and healing, energizing and activating, and stabilizing and sealing of your heart chakra filaments to the *front*.
- Continue to breathe through the front of your chest, and ask for the cleansing and clearing, repairing and healing, energizing and activating, and stabilizing and sealing of your heart chakra filaments to the *back*.

- Continue to breathe through the front of your chest, and ask for the cleansing and clearing, repairing and healing, energizing and activating, and stabilizing and sealing of your heart chakra filaments to the *right*.
- Continue to breathe through the front of your chest, and ask for the cleansing and clearing, repairing and healing, energizing and activating, and stabilizing and sealing of your heart chakra filaments to the *left*.
- Continue to breathe through the front of your chest, and ask for the cleansing and clearing, repairing and healing, energizing and activating, and stabilizing and sealing of your heart chakra filaments to the *bottom*.
- Continue to breathe through the front of your chest, and ask for the cleansing and clearing, repairing and healing, energizing and activating, and stabilizing and sealing of your heart chakra filaments to the *top*.
- Breathe in through the front of your chest and into your heart filaments *in all directions simultaneously,* asking them to resonate to their correct frequency.
- Ask your heart energy go to *the size that is appropriate* for functioning in your day-to-day life now. This is very important, because once you are out of your meditative state and back in the outside world, you don't want to be expanded out so far that you absorb everyone's rubbish or allow others to feed off you and leave you drained.
- Ask for all your chakras to be closed to the right size for you to function in your non-meditative, physical world.
- Strengthen your white light protection around your whole body, including your energy bodies.
- Bring your breathing up to your normal rate.
- Feel your weight upon the chair, and come back to physical awareness.
- Wriggle your fingers and toes, and when you're ready, open your eyes.
- If you need to write anything down, do it immediately—or else it will fade like a dream.

Until you have forgiven all that is not absolved, you will re-create distortion, damage, and breakage in your heart filaments. Commit to doing this exercise on a regular basis so you can reclaim your heart and get back into your life!

15. Heal Your Mind

Have you ever had times when you just can't think straight? Negative thinking and fault-finding can distort, damage, and break your brain filaments, similar to how excess emotion affects your heart filaments.

After you have repaired your heart filaments, you can draw this positive and loving energy up into your mind to help restore your mind filaments. This can help you prevent unpleasant thoughts and stories from repeating in your mind.

This is very important, because what you think about determines what you talk about—and in turn, what you do. Negative thinking creates negative speech and negative actions. *Where your mind goes, the energy flows!*

If you want your life to change, you need to change what you think, say, and do. Remember the definition of stupidity—doing the same thing over and over and expecting a different result. Changing your thinking and beliefs changes the seeds you've planted and gives you the opportunity to recreate the garden of your life with a positive foundation.

How to Use Your Heart Energy to Repair Your Mind Filaments

You need to do the repairing your heart filament exercise first, so you will need to allocate a reasonable amount of time to do this exercise—*the first part of this exercise is a repeat* of what you've done in the Heal Your Heart Filaments exercise.

- Clear yourself and your environment of all negativity.

- Protect yourself and the room you're in with the universal white light of positivity.
- Connect to your higher guidance and ask for assistance.
- Put yourself in a cone of light so any debris released is removed from you and sent to the light for transformation.
- Give yourself permission to heal.
- Uncross your arms and legs so that you have free energy flow through and around your body. The more open you are (within your cleared and protected space), the more completely you can heal yourself.
- Keep your breathing slow and steady, and go at your own pace. With your next breath, breathe in through the front of your chest and into your heart. For the whole of this exercise, continue to breathe through the front of your chest and into your heart.
- With your next breath, breathe in through the front of your chest, and expand your heart energy out to the *front*. Do this for three slow, steady breaths.

  o Repeat to the *back*
  o Repeat to the *right*
  o Repeat to the *left*
  o Repeat to the *bottom*
  o Repeat to the *top*

- With your next breath, breathe in through the front of your chest, and expand your heart energy *in all directions simultaneously*. Expand your heart chakra energy to about two meters past your body, and keep it stable. Do this for three slow, steady breaths.

Now you begin the "body" of your Healing Your Mind Filaments work.

- Breathe in through the front of your chest, and *breathe your heart energy up into your mind in your head*. Even though your mind is all-encompassing and permeates your whole body, you can access its blueprint most easily through your head and brain (just as you can access your soul most easily via your heart center).

- Keep your breathing slow and steady, and always go at your own pace. With your next breath, breathe in through the front of your chest, and expand your heart energy up into your mind and out to the *front* of your mind. Do this for three slow, steady breaths.
- With your next breath, breathe in through the front of your chest, and expand your heart energy up into your mind and out to the *back* of your mind. Do this for three slow, steady breaths.
- With your next breath, breathe in through the front of your chest, and expand your heart energy up into your mind and out to the *right* of your mind. Do this for three slow, steady breaths.
- With your next breath, breathe in through the front of your chest, and expand your heart energy up into your mind and out to the *left* of your mind. Do this for three slow, steady breaths.
- With your next breath, breathe in through the front of your chest, and expand your heart energy up into your mind and out to the *bottom* of your mind. Do this for three slow, steady breaths.
- With your next breath, breathe in through the front of your chest, and expand your heart energy up into your mind and out to the *top* of your mind. Do this for three slow, steady breaths.
- With your next breath, breathe in through the front of your chest, and expand your heart energy up into your mind and out *in all directions simultaneously*. Expand your mind energy to about two meters past your body, and keep it stable. Do this for three slow, steady breaths.
- Continue to breathe through the front of your chest and up into your mind. Ask for the cleansing and clearing, repairing and healing, energizing and activating, and stabilizing and sealing of your mind filaments to the *front*.

    o Repeat to the *back*
    o Repeat to the *right*
    o Repeat to the *left*
    o Repeat to the *bottom*
    o Repeat to the *top*

- Breathe in through the front of your chest, up into your mind, and into your mind filaments in *all directions simultaneously*, asking them to resonate at their correct frequency.

- Ask that your mind energy go to *the size that is appropriate* for functioning in your day-to-day life now. Again, this is very important, because once you are out of your meditative state and back in the outside world, you don't want to be expanded out so far that you absorb everyone's rubbish or allow others to feed off you and leave you drained.
- Ask for all your chakras to be closed to the right size for you to function in your non-meditative, physical world.
- Strengthen your white light protection around your whole body, including your energy bodies.
- Bring your breathing up to your normal rate.
- Feel your weight upon the chair and come back to physical consciousness.
- Wriggle your fingers and toes, and when you're ready, open your eyes.
- If you need to write anything down, do it immediately—or else it will fade like a dream.

Commit to do this exercise regularly, and weed the garden of your mind.

The more you take out the negative thoughts and beliefs from your mind, the easier it will be for you to stay positive and healthy.

If you leave the weeds to run rampant, it can get harder and harder to see your flowers.

Of course, make sure you don't plant more weeds. Keep cultivating flowers!

16. Integrate Your Heart and Mind

In the days of the ancients and the indigenous, decisions were always made by the feelings—the locations of water, suitable animals, trees bearing fruit, and plants with edible leaves and roots were innately known by following the feeling in the body. When to leave a given area because of changing seasons or a need to not "eat out" an area but allow it to naturally replenish was all in accordance with the feeling or inner knowing.

As humankind became more civilized and tried to exert its control over nature, the feeling became less strong. "Use it or lose it", they say! As we became housebound, determined to not head to better climes with the seasons, to farm animals rather than let them roam free, and grow crops rather than eat what was needed and allow the rest to return to the earth, the feeling became less strong again. What's more, we began to worship at the shrine of intellect. The mind and science grew, and the daydreaming child who "just knew what needed to be done" without any book learning got left behind.

Now we don't even restrict ourselves to our farmed foods in our local region, but have extended to importing and exporting all over the world. We don't even eat the energies of the foods that vibrate at the right frequency for the area we live in anymore. People in cold countries eat pineapples, and people in hot countries eat potatoes. If the vibration is not a match, it's not a match. We can justify it however we want (and regularly do), but we are not in alignment with what supports and maintains us—nor what supports and maintains the earth—anymore.

If we live in an area that doesn't have water, we dam the river, and then wonder why the earth responds with droughts and floods.

We chop down the trees to claim more and more land to farm our animals and crops, and then wonder why bushfires come. We mercilessly mine the minerals out of the ground, and then wonder why we get earthquakes. Did these events happen previously? Sure—just not with the magnitude and frequency they do now.

We've removed ourselves so far from our innate feeling and knowing that we now have whole societies that rely on drugs, therapists, and gymnasiums to deal with the stress of living the way we do. The more we're "in our heads," the more stress has to be "dealt with"—sooner or later.

It's not that thinking is bad. It's just that we think the same things over, and over, and over, and over …

How, then, can we get back to our inner knowing?

How can we get back to knowing what, when, and how to do something and then have our minds support and carry out the decisions (rather than making the decisions from here in the first place and then trying to make ourselves feel good about them)?

How can we get the dog back to wagging the tail?

How to Integrate Your Heart and Mind

Integrating your heart and mind allows you to feel and then follow through systematically. Rather than trying to ignore your mind—good luck with that!—give it its jobs to do that are initiated from your feeling and inner knowing.

If you have a child who is used to going to bed whenever it wants and you finally decide you've had enough of the inmate running the asylum, decide bedtime is 8:00 p.m. There's going to be a mutiny for a while as the child rebels. But you know that if you want sleep for everyone, an orderly and calm house, and any level of sanity, you have to follow through. After just a few short, challenging weeks, you'll get the results you choose—as long as you stick to your guns.

It's the same with your mind. In some areas, it's used to thinking and doing whatever it wants. It's been running your asylum, and it's time you were back in charge. It doesn't mean to ignore your mind. It means to decide from your feeling and inner knowing, then use your mind to action what you've decided. Get the order right!

Does it matter which order you put on your shoes or your socks? Yes! And it matters if you feel, and then think, or think, and then try and feel good about it.

Exercise

Begin by doing your Heal Your Heart and Mind Filament Exercise. By now, most people are keen to dedicate the time to their self-healing practices, because the results speak for themselves. Feel good for free! You can't ignore that! When you have cleansed and cleared, repaired and healed, energized and activated, and stabilized and sealed your mind filaments; expanded them in all directions simultaneously; and they resonate to their correct frequency:

- Mentally lift your mind down into your heart.
- Continue to breathe slowly and steadily, and allow your mind to merge with your heart center.
- Breathe three more slow, steady breaths (more if you wish).
- Ask that your integrated heart and mind energy go to *the size that is appropriate* for functioning in your day-to-day life now. Again, this is very important, because once you are out of your meditative state and back in the outside world, you don't want to be expanded out so far that you absorb everyone's rubbish or allow others to feed off you and leave you drained.
- Ask for all your chakras to be closed to the right size for you to function in your non-meditative, physical world.
- Resend you grounding cords down through the soles of your feet to the core of the earth.
- Strengthen your white light protection around your whole body, including your energy bodies.
- Bring your breathing up to your normal rate.
- Feel your weight upon the chair, and come back to physical consciousness.
- Wriggle your fingers and toes, and when you're ready, open your eyes.
- If you need to write anything down, do it immediately—or else it will fade like a dream.

In your everyday life, practice, practice, practice feeling your feelings, and then follow through and act on them, using the wonderful gift of your harnessed mind.

You may need to repeat this exercise regularly for a while until the child knows bedtime is 8:00 p.m.!

17. Fractals

If you photograph the side view of a mountain and take a section out of it, that section will show a similar likeness to the whole. If you take a photograph of a shoreline and take a section out of it, that section will show a similar likeness to the whole—and likewise, for a forest, river, and all aspects of nature.

All patterns in nature are "self-similar."

Self-similar sections or representations of the whole are called *fractals.*

Even with the master diamond blueprints of the body, there are diamonds inside diamonds inside diamonds—like Babushka dolls. Once a healer knows how to work with one diamond, they know how to work with most of them, because even though they all have different purposes and functions, *they all have the same basic structure.*

If you know how to work with one fractal, you know how to work with the others.

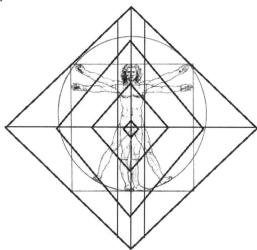

BASIC MASTER DIAMOND BLUEPRINT STRUCTURE

Are you wondering what this has got to do with you? This has *everything* to do with you:

- If you know how to repair your heart filaments, you already know how to repair your mind filaments.
- If you know how to repair your heart chakra, love, and forgiveness filaments, you also know how to repair your:

    o   Root chakra, abundance, and life direction filaments.
    o   Sex chakra, relationship, and intimacy filaments.
    o   Solar plexus chakra, self-esteem, and personal power filaments.
    o   Throat chakra, self-expression, and speaking your truth filaments.
    o   Third eye chakra, higher understanding, and discernment filaments.
    o   Crown chakra and spiritual connection filaments.

Do you follow me? Master the *Be In One Peace—Heal your Heal Filaments Method,* and you can apply it to any chakra or control center in your being!

This is *free gold!*

Are You Ready for More Gold?

Are there areas in your life where you have a bit of a challenge?

- Money?
- Career?
- The boss or co-workers?
- Health?
- Relationship?
- Friendships?
- Addictions?
- Weight?
- Body image?
- Self-esteem?
- Allowing compliments?

- Speaking in public?
- Singing?
- Painting?
- Spelling?
- Meditating?
- Letting go of your past?
- Forgiving someone?

Do you have at least one area where you're successful?

If you have even one area—do you breathe really well or make a cup of tea fit for a king?—you can master any other. They are fractals of you. If you already know how to work with one, you can apply your method to the others. Try it and see.

For example, if you're a gifted tea maker, how do you make tea?

- You know what equipment you need.
- You know what ingredients you need.
- You know what to do with the ingredients as well as when and how to do it.
- You have no doubt you can do it—your confidence is high.
- You actually do it and don't think about all the things that could go wrong or how embarrassed you'll feel if they do. You're aware of any risks, and if you muck up, you just fix it up and do it again.
- You've practiced it near perfectly, over and over—you have good experience

Are there more characteristics or steps than this? Probably—but you get the idea. If you approached everything with the same template, you'd master whatever you desired. The template you already use for the things you do well is the same template you should use for the areas where you've had challenges in the past. *Change those challenges into areas into which you now also do well.*

18. Wounded Healers

Rather than resolve the true cause of their issues, most people ignore the imbalances in their bodies and lives and find ways to either adapt or soldier on. We now have rampant use and abuse of medication, surgery, addiction, therapies, drugs, and quick-fix programs to cope with daily events.

Once you realize, however, that the imbalances are gifts, your whole world view changes forever. When your paradigm changes from one of suppressing pain and coping to looking for the gifts and being grateful for them, you start to steer your own bus again rather than sit in the back seat. You still have to find your way through the traffic, fill up with fuel, and get the bus serviced and cleaned; however, you're in a position of responsibility again.

The greatest wounds you have will be recognized as your greatest gifts when you accept the blessings within them.

Everyone comes into life with three wounds or challenges ahead of them. There is always balance in the universe—so equally that you will have three happy events to the same degree as your challenges. Remember to look for your fortunate events as well and not get overrun by the challenges.

Rather than waiting until you have resolved your issues to see what the gift was with your bright light of hindsight, begin to look for the gifts in your current challenges. *"Can't" usually means "won't."* If you can't see the gifts yet, ask yourself why you won't. I guarantee that it will be because you have to change something. Most of us are keen to change everything except ourselves. It's far easier to blame others and circumstances for our situations, but the truth is that we created our circumstances, and only by changing ourselves will we have lasting change around us.

Nature doesn't go in a straight line. Rivers take a meandering course from the mountains to the ocean—twisting this way and that around, over, and through obstacles. Our paths follow a similar route. Rather than get angry at the rocks in your stream, find a way around, over, or through them. Keeping safe doesn't work! There are always going to be rocks!

If you have an illness, be grateful for it. The location and nature of the illness tell you what you need to resolve and change in yourself.

If you have financial issues, spinal pain, blood disorders, or depression, be grateful for it. What are you learning? Have you discovered how to be resourceful and finds ways to earn money doing what you love? Do you even know what you love to do? Have you been stimulated to study and discover a new vocation or career? Where is the gift in your challenge? These issues are showing you that you need to heal your root chakra and manifestation beliefs, get orderly structure back in your life, and ground yourself—and get some exercise every day!

If you have relationship, hormone, or sex problems, be grateful. What are you learning? Are you noticing what people are reflecting back to you that you have hidden from yourself for so long? What are you doing about it? What do you intend to do about it? Are you learning to give love in order to receive it? Are you learning to love yourself rather than give all your love to another in the hope they will give it to you? Would you allow it in even if they did? You're being shown to heal your sex chakra, forgive your old hurts, let go of your rigidity, "go with the flow," and re-jig your boundaries.

If you don't feel good enough or have diabetes, gall bladder, liver, or stomach problems, be grateful. If you have body image issues, be grateful for them, too. What are you learning? Do you need to eat more nutritiously and honor the temple of your soul? Do you need to exercise your amazing machine? Are you loving yourself—regardless of what you look like? Or is your love conditional? Can you only love yourself if you are within a given weight range, have clear skin, and have an entourage of admirers with you? You're being shown to heal your solar plexus chakra, sort out your diet (come on! You know what to do!), take your power back, and resolve your anger issues once and for all.

If you have thyroid problems, neck pain, sore throats, or tonsillitis, be grateful. You're being shown to heal your throat chakra, speak up immediately instead of festering, turn your disappointments into stepping stones, and sing your own song.

If you have eye, ear, and nose issues and can't make a clear decision to save yourself, be grateful. You're being shown to heal your third eye chakra, look with your inner sight, listen to your inner voice, and think higher thoughts.

If you have headaches or psychological, mental, or hormonal problems, be grateful. You're being shown to heal your crown chakra, talk to God, listen to God, meditate, and align with your higher purpose.

To be grateful is to be great-ful—when you're grateful, you're full of greatness!

Be discerning. What has caused your issues? Be and do who and what is required to resolve it, and move on. Rather than trying to get back to where you were, strive to move forwards to higher ground. *Restoring something back to where it was is no use, because that's where the problem started in the first place! Stop trying to get your life back how it used to be! Move forward to where you choose it to be from here on.*

In learning how to resolve your own issues and illnesses, you discover things that can also help other people in their plights. It used to concern me that I had so many injuries from competitive sports and accidents and that I had to spend so much time, energy, and money learning how to resolve the consequences of them. I spent most of my adulthood healing the products of my childhood! However, it all turned out for the best, because I studied and experienced many healing methods and philosophies. I learnt what works and what doesn't! That's gold—not just gold for me, but also gold for the people who came to see me as a practitioner, because they were able to directly benefit from my search. If I hadn't had all the injuries and consequent health challenges, I may well have become just another book-learned practitioner and teacher rather than living up to my name.

What are your issues? Are you grateful for them yet? They are giving you gifts beyond all birthdays. Are you ready to unwrap them and enjoy your rewards that will result? Your issues show you precisely and succinctly what you need in order to love yourself, love others, and return to the oneness that your soul desires. It's all yours in this lifetime as soon as you allow it.

Look for the gift—it's in the present. It's right here, right now. You don't have to go to anywhere else to find it. It's not at a sacred site or guru conference. It's within you. Go within, and be in one peace.

About the Author:
Joanne, *The Messenger*

Joanne Messenger is just the person to write *Be In One Peace*. Most people know her as a chiropractor and Chiron healer, but she also has nearly thirty years of experience as a public speaker and course facilitator and was Australia's best-known teacher of Chiron philosophies and techniques.

Dr. Joanne Messenger was born the youngest of seven children—all girls, except for six boys—in Pingelly, Western Australia. Her mother was a nurse, so right from early beginnings, she was immersed in health care.

At an early age, one of her brothers was diagnosed as terminal. Being a nurse in the 1960s, her mother followed the medical route but got no happy result. Cortisone was the only easer. After an arduous path, her parents took her brother, Chris, to a chiropractor, where he was given spinal adjustments to restore function to his nerve system.

A *modern miracle* resulted!

In 1978, Joanne went to Chiropractic College in Melbourne to study this natural healing method that had worked wonders in her family.

Joanne was an excellent student, and her academic qualifications are impressive. She has a Bachelor's Degree in Applied Science (1982), a diploma from the National Board of Chiropractic Examiners (USA), an Excellence Award in Radiology, a Diploma of Sacro-Occipital Technique, Practitioner and Teacher Certificates in Chiron Healing, Certificate IV in Assessment and Workplace Training, is a certified Yoga (RYTA200) teacher, is certified in Neuro Linguistic

Programming (NLP) as applied to education, and has also studied Aromatherapy, Australian Bush Flower Essences; Essences of the Ancient Civilizations, Pleiadean Light Work, and Pranic Healing.

Dr. Joanne is one of the founding members of Chiron Healing, past Principal of the Australian Energy School of Chiron, past Vice President of the International Association of Chiron Healers, Inc., and past treasurer of S.O.T.O. A/Asia Ltd.

Joanne studied firsthand with Master Chiron and compiled the manuals and teaching programs for Chiron Healing. Philosophical differences led to a parting of the ways, and *Be In One Peace* and *Blueprint Healing* evolved.

Joanne has taught the philosophies and techniques of energy and healing throughout Australia and the world.

Appendix

Love Mist

Be In One Peace™ *Love Mist* is also known as *Life Purpose Mist*. It contains aromatherapy practitioner-grade 100 percent pure essential oils which have been reconnected to their ancient source and a botanical essence in purified water, which assists you to connect with your higher self. These are:

- *Lavender,* which helps you relax and achieve your aims. It also helps repair minor damage to your lines of energy.
- *Patchouli,* which helps your main line of energy and where it enters the top of your head as the structure of your crown chakra or crown energy centre.
- *Rose,* which helps you open your heart and trust yourself and your own wisdom.
- *Cymbidium Orchid Royal Fair Krista,* which helps you connect, manifest your dreams, and see your own beauty and light.

Love Mist helps you connect with your higher self and life purpose. Life is so much easier when you find, know, and live your own path. Use it to manifest your higher goals rather than go around in the circles of your ego.

You can also use it as a room spray at home, work, or in classrooms where it is for everyone's highest good to live and work to their potential.

Peace Mist

Be In One Peace™ Peace Mist is a blend of 100 percent pure aromatherapy practitioner-grade oils which have been connected back to their source and botanical essences in purified water, which assist you to clear negative energy. It contains:

- *Lavender* is often reputed as the panacea of all ills. It might be a faster job to list the few things it doesn't do rather than the extensive list of things it does. It helps with everything from clearing negativity to healing wounds and burns, helps bonding and relationships, and lifts depression and moods. It is a beautiful aroma which is almost universally recognized.
- *Frankincense* helps you connect to your spirit. It is a base note aroma which also has an appealing feeling.
- *Rose* is known as the oil of the heart. It is most known for its association with love and all matters of the heart. It fits with the old adage that says, "There is no situation known to man that enough love cannot heal." Rose is one of nature's best tools to help in the healing of those situations. Good rose oils are particularly expensive, but absolutely beautiful.
- *Cordyline terminalis botanical essence (also known as Ti)* has proven to be an effective defense against negative energies directed at a person and has been used by the Hawaiians and Polynesians for centuries to lift spells and curses.
- *Acorn botanical essence* is the fruit of the oak tree and has been used through the ages for clearing and protecting the aura. It is also an antidote for some poisons; an aid for poor digestion, colic, diarrhea, and dysentery; and is used to help contact higher beings.
- *Amethyst vibrational essence* is used for clearing, protection, and energizing.

Peace Mist is regularly used in the home and at work. It helps family, workmates, and customers to relax, be in good moods, and be themselves. This creates a clearer environment for everyone.

Aura Cleanser Body Washes

You can use *Be In One Peace™ Aura Cleanser Body Washes* in your bath or shower daily to clean your physical body and aura simultaneously. These are especially good for children. They:

- Have no animal content
- Have no artificial colors
- Have no artificial fragrances
- Are not tested on animals
- Are eco-friendly
- Are in recyclable containers

Be In One Peace™ Aura Cleanser body washes are a sodium lauryl sulphate-free liquid soap with blends of:

- 100 percent aromatherapy practitioner-grade pure essential oils
- Cordyline terminalis
- Acorn botanical essences
- Amethyst vibrational essence

If your energy is particularly congested or blocked, use an aura cleanser on a loofah for deeper cleansing. It's revitalizing!

Glossary

Affirmation: An affirmation is a positive statement stated as a fact to bring about a desired change—e.g., "I am confident," "I am healthy," or "I am flexible."

It is best to state your affirmations as "I am" rather than "I want," because if you affirm, "I want something," you get exactly that—to keep on wanting it, rather than having or being it.

Aura: Your aura is the subtle emanation of light surrounding and permeating your body. It contains the Master Diamond Blueprints for your physical body as well as the mental and emotional bodies. Sensitive people see the aura as moving colors and structural lines of silver.

All living creatures have an aura. It can be measured using Super Conducting Quantum Interference Devices and photographed with Kirlian Photography.

Australian Bush Flower Essences. Australian Bush Flower Essences are made from Australian plants in their natural, pristine environment. They act as catalysts to resolve your negative beliefs and give you the clarity and resolve to commit to your goals.

Botanical essences: Botanical essences are made by soaking flowers in pure water, which imbues the therapeutic properties of the flower and plant into the water. You can administer them orally or topically for their therapeutic benefits.

Chakra: *Chakra* is a Sanskrit word meaning "wheel." The chakras are the spinning wheels of energy which feed the nervous and endocrine or hormonal systems of the body. This in turn affects all the muscles, tissues, and organs of the body. There are nine major and multiple minor chakras.

Chiropractic: Chiropractic works by making adjustments to the spine to correct subluxations. Subluxations are misalignments of the spinal vertebrae, which interfere with the nerves as they exit from the spinal cord. This interference results in malfunction of whatever is controlled by those nerves (i.e., the corresponding muscles and organs), resulting in pain and disease.

Emotional body: Your emotional body is in your aura, between your mental and physical body. It is the blueprint for your emotions and feelings.

Essential oils: Pure essential oils are the aromatic liquid from plants. They are referred to as the hormones of the plant. They generally extracted from various flowers, fruits, leaves, grasses, and roots by distillation. They help with many physical conditions as well as balancing the emotions. They are particularly good for home help in between visits.

Etheric body: The etheric body is the subtle body closest to your physical body. It is your energy blueprint, and it determines the physical functioning of your body.

Earthbound soul: An earthbound soul is a being whose body had died but whose soul hasn't moved on to the light (i.e., they have stayed close to the earth instead of continuing their journey). When an earthbound soul is within your aura, you can experience all sorts of symptoms, similar to a confusing personality change. You may get the urge to smoke when you're a nonsmoker or eat things you wouldn't normally go for; your thoughts and actions are influenced by the soul that is overriding your blueprint. Some earthbound souls are simply unaware. They may not know to move on to the light, or they may not even realize they are dead. This is common if they haven't been sick or had any warning they were going to die, or if they were in an accident or blown up at war and their body is not recognizable for them to work out what's going on.

Some simply don't move on to the light because they firmly believe there is no life after death, and they don't even look.

Some don't move on because they are too attached to something (typically money or physical possessions) or someone (an excessively clingy or codependent relationship).

Mental body: Your mental body is one of the subtle bodies within your aura and is the blueprint for your beliefs.

Over-soul: An over-soul is the universal mind, spirit, or energy that animates, motivates, and unifies a group or family.

Protection: (see *Psychic protection*).

Psychic protection: and energetic protection are often used interchangeably. They simply refer to guarding yourself from absorbing aberrant energies and frequencies that don't sustain you (such as aberrant sounds, sights, smells, emotions of others, earthbound souls, or step-out step-ins).

Step-out step-in: A step-out step-in is an earthbound soul who steps out of your aura when you clear and then steps right back in again. This being/person has no intention of moving on. They are quite happy to be disruptive to the person they are hooked into. Just because a person dies doesn't mean they are suddenly nice or wise. Just as there are disruptive people who are living, people can be equally disruptive when they're out of their bodies.

Subluxation: A subluxation is a misalignment of a vertebra which interferes with the nerve system, resulting in less than optimal health and well-being and dis-ease.

Universal white light: *(see White light).*

Vibrational essences: My vibrational essences are made from gemstones. I soak them in pure water under given conditions. The properties of the stone are imbued into the water, and the water is made usable for the gemstones' therapeutic properties.

White light: has all the colors of the spectrum within it—red, orange, yellow, green, blue, indigo, and violet. It is often referred to as the Universal White Light of Protection.